Arthur Schopenhauer

Select essays of Arthur Schopenhauer

Arthur Schopenhauer

Select essays of Arthur Schopenhauer

ISBN/EAN: 9783337731595

Printed in Europe, USA, Canada, Australia, Japan

Cover: Foto ©ninafisch / pixelio.de

More available books at **www.hansebooks.com**

SELECT ESSAYS

OF

ARTHUR SCHOPENHAUER.

TRANSLATED BY

GARRITT DROPPERS AND C. A. P. DACHSEL.

"He took the suffering human race;
　He read each wound, each weakness clear;
He struck his finger on the place,
　And said, 'Thou ailest here and here.'"

Milwaukee:
SENTINEL COMPANY, PRINTERS.
1881.

CONTENTS.

BIOGRAPHICAL SKETCH,	9
THE MISERY OF LIFE,	29
METAPHYSICS OF LOVE,	55
GENIUS,	106
ÆSTHETICS OF POETRY,	144
EDUCATION,	170

PREFACE.

"WHOEVER wishes to understand my philosophy thoroughly," says Schopenhauer, "must read every line of my works;" for many of his apparently paradoxical assertions are really but logical deductions from his system of philosophy. The following essays, therefore, give the reader but a general insight into his characteristics. However, we have selected those essays which are most unique and complete in themselves.

We have adhered as closely as possible to the literal, even retaining peculiarities of style.

We hope that this little work will serve to eradicate many of the superstitions current about Schopenhauer.

The short biographical sketch preceding the essays is mainly an excerpt from Gwinner's "Life of Schopenhauer."

MILWAUKEE, May 21, 1881.

BIOGRAPHICAL SKETCH.

ARTHUR SCHOPENHAUER, the eldest child and only son of Henry Floris Schopenhauer, a wealthy merchant, and of Johanna Schopenhauer, the well-known authoress, was born on the 22d of February, 1788, at Danzig, then a small German free-state.

Arthur's father was not a common man. That rare faculty of combining the pride of the aristocrat with the enterprising spirit of the merchant, he possessed in an eminent degree. Though devoted to business, he by no means neglected his mental culture, reading with especial interest the works of Voltaire. During a sojourn of several years in France and England, he became thoroughly familiar with the language and customs of those countries. So prepossessed was he in favor of the state and family life of the English, that for a long time he meditated settling down among them. His home was furnished with English comfort. Daily he read an English and a French newspaper, and induced his son at an early age to do the same. And Arthur followed the paternal advice to the end of his life. He himself says of his father: "He was a strict, passionate man, but of irreproachable rectitude and fidelity, and endowed with an excellent insight into commercial matters. How much I am indebted to him, I can hardly express in words. All the advantages — liberty, leisure, and all the resources to follow the career for which alone I was born — I owe solely to him. They enabled me to prosecute exclusively, for a number of years, studies which are the last to yield pecuniary reward, and to follow researches and meditations of the most difficult kind. Therefore, as long as I live, I will ever cherish in my heart the inexpressible merits and provident care of my best father, and keep his memory sacred."

At the age of thirty-eight, the elder Schopenhauer selected for marriage Johanna Trosiener, the daughter of a Danzig senator. Sagacious, witty, talkative, and not without personal charms, she afterwards gained a reputation as a novelist and writer of travels. Her husband was twenty years her senior.

From his father, Arthur inherited the passionate temperament, the proud, inflexible spirit, the keen sense of order, and the burning love of truth and justice; from his mother, the vivacity and acuteness of the intuitive powers, sagacity, and facility of linguistic expression: Mother and son were both brilliant conversers. When, in 1793, the small Republic yielded to Prussian power, the parents fled to Hamburg, where their stay was interrupted by frequent trips on the Continent. In the course of these travels, they became acquainted with many famous contemporaries,—Klopstock, Tischbein, Reimarus, Baron Staël, Sieveking, Lady Hamilton, and Lord Nelson.

Arthur's education as a man of the world was the secondary object of these travels, which his father never lost sight of. When, in 1797, they made a pleasure trip to France and England, the boy, who had hitherto received instruction in a private school, was left with a friend at Havre. Says Schopenhauer: "After we had seen Paris, I stayed over two years at Havre, where I was educated with the son of the house, who was of the same age, so that, if possible, I might become a thorough Frenchman. We were instructed by private tutors in all the branches and accomplishments adapted to that tender age. We were grounded in the French language, and also in the rudiments of Latin. In that friendly city, situated at the mouth of the Seine, and on the seashore, I passed the happiest days of my childhood."

When he returned without a companion to Hamburg, he had almost forgotten his native language, and could but gradually again accustom himself to its harsh sounds. He then entered Runge's private institution, where the sons of the most respectable families were his schoolmates. At this time there arose in him a love for science, which was very displeasing to his father, to whom a scholar's career seemed inseparable from poverty; accordingly, Arthur's father had recourse to the following stratagem. He availed himself of the boy's longing for his beloved friend in Havre, and of his equally potent desire to see the world, by giving him the choice either to immediately enter the gymnasium, or, forever resigning a scholar's career, to engage in a mercantile pursuit, after enjoying a few years of travel. Arthur, then fifteen years of age, could not resist the temptation. During a visit to England, he was put into the boarding-school of a parson at Wimbledon, where he spent several months under his care, while his parents made an excursion to the Highlands. He there laid the foundation to his future intimacy with English language and literature, but also to his hatred of English bigotry. The gay manners of the French were more congenial to him than English reserve, so that in the colder atmosphere he found himself suddenly thrown back on his own resources. However, he was allowed to devote his time to the fine arts and to gymnastic exercises, flute-playing, singing, drawing, riding, fencing, and dancing.

On their return to Hamburg, in 1805, Arthur, true to his pledge, entered a mercantile business, which was utterly repulsive to him. "I entered," says he, "the business of a respectable Hamburg merchant and senator; but there never lived a worse apprentice than myself. My whole nature was opposed to this occupation; with something else ever in my mind, I neglected my duties, and was, day after day, intent but upon gaining time which I might devote at home to my books, or during which I could, at least, revel in thoughts and fantasies. Besides, I always had books hidden in the office, and, whenever I was not watched, I perused them. When the famous founder of phrenology, Gall, was delivering lectures in Hamburg, I constantly attended them, daily deceiving my superiors with cunning pretexts. In addition to this, a deep depression of spirits made me disobedient and burdensome to others, partly because, in place of the continual diversions, to which my journeys had accustomed me, I was bound to a hated occupation; partly, because I became more and more convinced that I had taken a wrong course of life, a mistake I wholly despaired of correcting."

But this did not continue long. The sudden death of his father threw him into the saddest mood, not far removed from true melancholy. Although he was then his own master, as his mother allowed him to do as he pleased, he did not at once leave the office; excessive grief had destroyed the energy of his mind, and he hesitated to break his promise; besides, he considered himself too far advanced in life to learn the ancient languages. But his work daily grew more intolerable to him. After two years wholly useless to him, he broke out into violent lamentations to his mother over his frustrated life-purpose, and over the irreparable loss of his youthful powers devoted to fruitless labor.

During this time his mother was living at Weimar, whither she had moved after the death of her husband. She mingled with the gay society of the place, and in her *salon* were gathered all the *literati* of the day. Feeling the necessity of a change in the occupation of her son, she consulted her friend Fernow, who advised her to send Arthur to the University. At the receipt of his mother's letter granting his request, he burst into tears. His resolution was at once taken. In the beginning of 1807 he entered the then flourishing gymnasium at Gotha, but, being entirely ignorant of the classical languages, he could participate in those studies only which did not require a knowledge of those languages. But a dangerous habit of indulging in sarcastic remarks forced him to leave the gymnasium before the close of the year. On his return to Weimar, he lived for two years with Passow, an able classical scholar, who prepared him for the University. Towards the end of 1809, being now of age, he matriculated at the University of Gœttingen as a student of medicine. That these years at the University were spent to advantage, Schopenhauer's own words will attest: "After I had obtained some, though but superficial, knowledge of myself and of philosophy, I changed my resolution, and, discarding medicine, devoted myself exclusively to philosophy. However, the time which I had devoted to the former was by no means wasted; for up to this time I had attended but such lectures as are useful to the philosopher as well. I applied myself diligently to scientific studies, from which my intercourse with other students could by no means deter me, for my more mature age, my richer experience, and my fundamentally different nature, led me at all times to isolation and solitude. Though I attended the lectures regularly, I still had a great deal of time to read, which I devoted especially to Kant and Plato. I attended G. E. Schulze's lectures on logic, metaphysics, and psychology; Heeren's, on history; Blumenbach's, on natural history, mineralogy, physiology, and comparative anatomy; and many others."

In 1811, he continued his studies at Berlin, where Wolf was lecturing on Greek literature and antiquities, Lichtenstein on zoölogy, Fichte on philosophy. In Berlin, too, he would have remained two years, had not the war of 1813 driven him away; which he deplored the more, because he was preparing to obtain the degree of Ph. D. from the Berlin University. For this reason he had commenced to write the treatise, " On the Four-fold Root of the Principle of Sufficient Reason." It was his intention to return home to Weimar, but he was so much displeased with certain domestic relations that he sought another place of refuge. In Rudolstadt, beautifully situated in a valley, he spent the summer in completing the dissertation commenced at Berlin. But the dreariness of winter soon drove him back to Weimar, and here, according to his own account, there occurred one of the happiest events of his life : "For," says he, "that truly great ornament of our century and of the German nation, the great Goethe, whose name will forever be on the lips of men, deemed me worthy of his friendship and of intimate intercourse. For before this, I was known to him but by sight; but after he had looked over my treatise, he came to me of his own accord and asked me whether I would like to study his theory of colors. He promised to assist me in every way, so that this theme might become the subject of our conversation, whether or no I would agree with his opinions. Several days afterward, he sent me his own apparatus and the instruments necessary to the production of the phenomena of colors, and later, he himself showed me the more difficult experiments, highly delighted that my mind, blinded by no preconceived opinions, recognized the truth of his doctrine, which, to the present day, from causes which it is out of place to mention here, has been denied consent and due acknowledgment. When we became more intimate, our conversation was not restricted to the theory of colors, but we discussed, for hours at a time, all possible philosophical topics. From this intimate intercourse with him I have profited much."

In the spring of 1814, he betook himself to Dresden, to continue his studies, but more especially, to work out the system of philosophy which was already forming in his mind. He also developed his theory of colors, which was published in 1816. Two years later, he brought to a close his philosophical system, which had almost uninterruptedly engaged his attention for five years, and upon which his reputation substantially rests. Soon after, he sought recreation in a journey to Italy. He visited Venice, Bologne, Florence; lastly Rome, where he stayed nearly four months, and enjoyed himself in contemplating the monuments of antiquity, as well as modern works of art. After an absence of eleven months, he returned to Dresden, and subsequently to Berlin, where he delivered a course of lectures at the University on his system of philosophy. After a few months they were discontinued for want of attendance, while people even crawled through the windows to listen to Hegel, whose fame was then at its height. Thus two years (1820–22) passed, in which, though his ambition did not receive the least encouragement, he crystallized and extended his scientific knowledge. But the atmosphere of Berlin threatened to suffocate him. In order to retain confidence in himself and his calling, in the beginning of May, 1822, he traveled to Switzerland, after making his will. He enjoyed a splendid summer in the Alps, and in the fall continued his journey to Florence, where he spent the winter. Upon his return from Italy to Munich, he lay sick all winter. The single ray of sunshine which lightened those dark days was a distinction which the Academy of that city conferred upon him. In a pamphlet published by the Academy on the progress of the theory of the mechanism of the senses, himself and Purkinje were the only ones mentioned.

The year 1826 ended a five years' lawsuit with a spinster by the name of Marquet, who had sued Schopenhauer for injuries she claimed she had sustained when he expelled her from his premises. The court decided in favor of the plaintiff, and he was compelled to support her for the rest of her life. Twenty years after, he wrote on her death certificate, "*Obit anus, abit onus.*" The manifest injustice, the humiliation, and disappointment at the issue of this "confounded" suit struck him more heavily than the material loss he incurred. Hardly entered into manhood, he had experienced its bitter lessons, although he sought neither money, nor friendship, nor honors; in a word, none of the prizes which it is the ambition of others to win. His inner life seems to have been entirely devoid of growth during this period; with woeful reflections, he already turns his eye to the past. On his thirty-eighth birthday, the days of the lawsuit, he writes the following reflection: "Objects are for the mind only what the lyre is for the plectrum. At the time my mental activity was at its height, when, by favoring circumstances, the hour came in which my brain was at its greatest tension, my eye could strike what object soever it listed — it spoke revelations to me. But now, being old, *che va mancando l' entusiasmo celeste*, I can stand before the Madonna of Raphael, and she tells me nothing."

But Schopenhauer, perhaps prone by nature to see the misery of the world in the darkest colors, was, in spite of his numerous practical failures and misfortunes, by no means a gloomy hermit. His frequent travels, his profound remarks on men and things, and his occasional love affairs, proving that he took a keen interest in human matters, corroborate the opinion of the *Revue Contemporaine:* "Schopenhauer is not like other philosophers: he is a philosopher who has seen the world."

On Nov. 1st, 1818, he writes in his journal: "He who is suddenly transplanted into a wholly strange land or city, where there is a very different manner of living, or even another language, feels like one who has plunged into cold water: he comes in contact with a temperature very different from his own; he feels a powerful, superior, outside influence which makes him uneasy. He is in a foreign element where he cannot move with ease; besides, because everything strikes him in a new and conspicuous light, he is afraid of being as conspicuous to others. But as soon as he is somewhat calmed, and has accustomed himself to the environment, and accepted its temperature somewhat, he feels, like the one in cold water, extraordinarily well; he becomes assimilated to the element. He is then no longer forced to occupy himself with his person, and directs his whole attention to the surroundings, to which, by the very objective, neutral contemplation, he now feels himself superior, instead of being depressed by it as before." In such high spirits he entered the land of beauty; he was neither born nor educated to be a pedant. Our philosopher, and another famous pessimist, the author of "Childe Harold," happened to be in Venice at the same time. An almost ungovernable "will to live" drove both through the same heights and depths — how else could they have represented it with such matchless power? Byron, — who at that time created that work of which Goethe says that it is the product of boundless genius, misanthropic to bitterest cruelty, philanthropic to depths of sweetest emotion, — writes, at the close of the Carnival, to Tom Moore: "I will work the mine of my youth to the last veins of the ore, and then, 'good-night.' I have lived, and am content." Even in old age, a tender mood, otherwise wholly foreign to him, overcame Schopenhauer when he spoke of Venice, where the magic arms of love ensnared him for a time, until an inner voice commanded him to tear himself away and continue his journey alone. Byron was in the habit, when the weather permitted, of taking his gondola to the Lido, where he kept his horses, in order to take his daily ride along the beach to Malamocco. On one of these trips he met Schopenhauer, a meeting which the latter remembered the more as his Venetian mistress aroused his jealousy by the lively interest she took in Byron's splendid appearance. The philosopher and the poet chanced to become acquainted in this manner: They were riding in gondolas, accompanied by their mistresses, who were fast friends and introduced the gentlemen to each other. At this time, Chateaubriand and Leopardi were in Italy, so that the four great pessimists could have had the best opportunity to hold a congress of pessimists along with the congress of Verona.

At Berlin, in 1826, he was in such a gloomy frame of mind that the idea of marrying, often rejected, came to him with redoubled force. When he had given up the hope of obtaining a professorship, he intended to marry and move into a country town — to cut off every opportunity to purchase books, a necessity, to gratify which seemed seriously to threaten his economy at Berlin in case he married. However, he soon rid himself of these illusions. In one of his works he says: "What people commonly call fate, is usually nothing but their own folly; evil deeds are atoned for in the next world; foolish deeds, in this." The older he became, the more easily could he choose his course, the more reasons he amassed in favor of his bachelordom. He felt in himself neither the ability, nor the calling, nor the courage, to assume the burdens and responsibilities of married life. Intellectuality was at all times preponderant in him. From youth, his dreams of happiness were always founded upon scenes of repose and solitude. If his real life, he thought, had been the cardinal affair of his existence and the source of his enjoyments, he would have done well to marry; but, as his life, on the contrary, was an ideal, an intellectual one, he dared not do it; for one must be sacrificed to the other. A man who, from what reason soever, has departed from the natural course of life, durst never marry. He considered his inheritance a sacred treasure, entrusted to him to solve the problem imposed upon him by nature, to be, for himself and humanity, that for which she destined him; otherwise, he would be useless to humanity, and, perhaps, lead the most miserable existence a man of his stamp ever led. Therefore, he considered it the most ungrateful and unworthy misuse of so rare a lot, if, in the so often disappointed expectation of a life richer in enjoyments, he would expend, perhaps, half of his income in "bonnets and dresses." He was of the opinion that the more reasonable and wiser a man is, the worse he fares in a union with the "unreasonable half of mankind;" and justly, as this union on his part is greater folly. Finally, who has reached the age of forty without burdening himself with wife and children must have, indeed, learned little, if he would then marry. Such a man appeared to him like one who has tramped three-fourths of a distance, and then wishes to purchase a ticket for the whole trip. He took a delight in finding similar maxims in the works of great predecessors. He loved to appeal to Bacon,— "Essay on marriage and single life,"—who says: "He that hath wife and children, hath given hostages to Fortune; for they are impediments to great enterprises, either of virtue or mischief. Certainly, the best works, and of greatest merit for the public, have proceded from the unmarried, or childless men, which, both in affection and means, have endowed the public." His true companion was philosophy, of which he beautifully says: "Philosophy is a lofty Alpine road, to which there leads but a steep path, over sharp stones and pricking thorns; the path is lonely, and becomes more desolate the higher you ascend; and who passes over it, must know no trembling, but forsake all, and calmly make his own way through the cold snow. Often, he suddenly stands on the verge of an abyss, and sees the green valley below; dizziness takes possession of him; but he must hold his ground, though he waste his life-blood in the effort to cling to the rocks. But, as a reward, he soon sees the world beneath him; its deserts and morasses vanish; its unevenness is leveled; its discords do not reach him; its rotundity is revealed. He himself always stands in pure, cool Alpine air, and sees the sun, when black night still hangs heavy over the country below."

In 1831, a cholera epidemic drove him from Berlin to Frankfort-on-the-Main, where, with few interruptions, he lived until his death. Shortly after his arrival at that city, which he called "too small for a great, too great for a small city, and, on the whole, a nest of gossip," he fell sick, and became so ill-humored that, for weeks, he spoke to no human soul. This was caused partly by the neglect of his works, which he had offered in vain to his contemporaries, and partly by his failing to secure an academic chair. For nearly a generation he lived among the shop-keepers and money-makers of this city, undisturbed and unknown, or merely referred to as "the son of the famous Johanna Schopenhauer."

The disadvantages accompanying genius, which he has so drastically described in his own works, were felt by Schopenhauer perhaps more than by any other of those rare intellects. Nature did her best to isolate his heart, endowing it with suspicion, irritability, vehemence, and pride, in a measure almost incapable of being united with the *mens aequa* of the philosopher. He inherited from his father a dread bordering on mania, against which he struggled all his life, with all the will-power at his command, and which, at times, on the most trivial occasions, overcame him with such power that he saw the most improbable evils before him. A fertile imagination frequently magnified this native tendency to an incredible degree. When but a child of six, his parents, returning home from a walk one evening, found him in utter despair, imagining that they had deserted him forever. When a youth, he was tortured by all sorts of imaginary evils and quarrels. While studying at Berlin, he fancied himself consumptive. In Verona, the fixed idea seized him that he had taken poisoned snuff. He never entrusted himself to the razor of a barber. He always carried a small leather cup with him, in order to avoid catching contagious diseases when drinking in public places. Bacon's saying, that all suspicion is founded on ignorance, he rejected, and thought, with Chamfort, "The beginning of wisdom is fear of men."

The same man, whose highest tenet of morals was, that he is the best man who makes least distinction between himself and others, and he the worst who makes most, was possessed of the deep, unwavering conviction that starry spaces separated him from those with whom he ought to mingle, and whom he ought to love.

The boy, gazing with astonished eyes upon this life, maintained by hunger and love; the youth, timidly approaching it, hiding his own inner world; the man, opposing it as a hostile stranger; the old man, at last, beholding it far beneath him, and his fiery, clear eye chilled in cold resignation;—all this must be seen, to make ethically intelligible to us his sad loneliness, the desolate waste of his existence, his unspeakable scorn of men, the hardness of the pride with which he surrounded his heart as with a coat of mail.

His reading was, perhaps, less extensive than

many would suppose. But his incomparable discrimination in selecting passages from authors, and in bringing these in on the proper occasion, enabled him to cull from the remotest fields of literature whatever was necessary to his purposes; so that his books, apart from their intrinsic merits, are a repository of splendid quotations from a wide range of writers.

A habit of reading the ancient writers for two hours a day, made him almost as familiar with Greek and Latin as with his mother-tongue. Horace and Seneca were his favorite Latin authors; David Hume, his favorite English; Helvetius, his favorite French author. He took a deep interest in the ascetic and mystic literature of all times and climes. "Buddha, Eckhart, and myself," he says, in one of his posthumous fragments, "in the main teach the same." Pieces which never ceased to delight him, were the 105th Epistle of Seneca; the beginning of Hobbes' De Cive; Machiavelli's Principe; the speech of Polonius to Laertes, in Hamlet; the maxims of Gracian, Shenstone, Klinger, and the French moralists. Throughout his life he was fond of the great poets, especially Shakespeare and Goethe, and, next, Calderon and Byron, whose pessimistic Cain naturally pleased him most. Petrarch, Burns, and Bürger, he gave a high rank. Second-rate poets he never read. As the Italians boast of their four poets, he spoke with pleasure of four romances, "Don Quixote," "Tristram Shandy,"

"Heloise," and "Wilhelm Meister," thus ascribing one to each nation, with the exception of the Italians; "for Boccaccio," he says, "relates nothing but scandals." The "Wilhelm Meister" he calls an intellectual romance, whose key-note is the idea that in life we fare like the wanderer, before whom, as he advances, objects take shapes different from those which they show from afar, and, as it were, transform themselves at his approach; so that we find something very different, nay, better than what we sought; instead of pastimes and happiness, instruction and insight; a lasting and true good, instead of a perishable and seeming good.

Schopenhauer, to some extent, imitated Kant's mode of living. He was not an early riser, as he believed that a long sleep was necessary for a brain-worker. Summer and winter, he arose between seven and eight o'clock. He prepared his own coffee. During the morning hours, he wished to be alone, even requiring his servant to keep out of his sight. In the latter part of his life, when his reputation was growing, he received visitors toward noon. He dined at one o'clock. His appetite was so hearty that he even held it among his vices, but consoled himself with the fact that Kant and Goethe were also huge feeders, and that he was the more moderate drinker. He liked to converse at meals, but, for want of fit company, he usually contemplated his neighbors. For a time, he daily laid a *ducat* on the table, without his table-companions understanding his motive. At last, when asked about it, he replied that he would give it to the poor, if the officers dining with him would but once start a more earnest conversation than about horses, dogs, and women. After dinner, he went home, took a short siesta, and spent the earlier part of the afternoon in reading light literature. Towards evening he went into the open air, and always chose the most secluded paths. His gait was rapid and of youthful elasticity to the end of his life. He often indulged in the eccentricities common to persons of a sanguine temperament, as, for instance, striking the ground with his bamboo cane, and uttering inarticulate sounds. His supper, taken between eight and nine o'clock, consisted of cold meats and half a bottle of light wine. Wine easily excited him, so that he became lively after the second glass. To beer he had a decided aversion.

The second volume of "The World as Will and Representation," was published in 1843. His last, and most popular work "*Parerga and Paralipomena*," upon which he spent six years of incessant labor, appeared in 1850.

He died on the 20th of September, 1860. According to his own direction, he was buried in an oak coffin. A square slab, with the inscription, *Arthur Schopenhauer*, marks his grave in the cemetery at Frankfort-on-the-Main. When asked by his friend and biographer, Dr. Gwinner, where he wished to lie, he replied, "Anywhere; they will find me."

THE MISERY OF LIFE.

HAVING awakened to life from the night of unconsciousness, the will finds itself as an individual in an endless and boundless world, among innumerable individuals, all striving, suffering, erring; and, as though passing through an uneasy dream, it hurries back to the old unconsciousness. Until then, however, its desires are boundless, its claims inexhaustible, and every satisfied wish begets a new one. No satisfaction possible in the world could suffice to still its longings, put a final end to its craving, and fill the bottomless abyss of its heart. Consider, too, what gratifications of every kind man generally receives: they are, usually, nothing more than the meagre preservation of this existence itself, daily gained by incessant toil and constant care, in battle against want, with death forever in the van. Everything in life indicates that earthly happiness is destined to be frustrated, or to be recognized as an illusion. The germs for this lie deep in the nature of things. Accordingly, the life of most of us proves sad and short. The comparatively happy are usually only apparently so, or are, like long-lived persons, rare exceptions,—left as a bait for the rest.

Life proves a continued deceit, in great as well as small matters. If it makes a promise, it does not keep it, unless to show how unworthy the coveted object was; thus, sometimes hope, sometimes what was hoped for, deludes us. If it gave, it was but to take away. The fascination of distance presents a paradise, vanishing like an optical delusion, when we have allowed ourselves to be enticed thither. Happiness, accordingly, lies always in the future, or in the past; and the present is to be compared to a small, dark cloud which the wind drives over the sunny plain; before it and behind it, all is bright; it alone casts a shadow. The present, therefore, is forever unsatisfactory; the future, uncertain; the past, irrecoverable. Life, with its hourly, daily, weekly, and yearly, small, greater, and great adversities, with its disappointed hopes, and mishaps foiling all calculation, bears so plainly the stamp of something we should get disgusted with, that it is difficult to comprehend how any one could have mistaken this, and been persuaded that life was to be thankfully enjoyed, and we to be happy. Much more, that everlasting delusion and disappointment, as well as the constitution of life throughout, appear as though they were intended and calculated to awaken the conviction that nothing whatever is worthy of our striving, driving, and wrestling,—that all goods are naught, the world bankrupt at all ends, and life a business that does not pay expenses,—in order that our will may turn away from it.

The manner in which this nothingness of all objects of the will makes itself manifest and comprehensible to the intellect rooted in the individual, is, in the first place, *time*. Time is the form, by means of which this nothingness of things appears as transitoriness; since through the latter all our enjoyments and pleasures come to nought, and we afterward ask, in astonishment, what has become of them. This nothingness itself, accordingly, is the only thing *objective* about time, that is, that which corresponds to it in the existence of things *per se;* consequently, that of which it is the expression. For this very reason, time is the *apriori* necessary form of all our perceptions; in it, all, even we ourselves, must be represented. Accordingly, in the first place, our life resembles a payment which we receive in nothing but copper-pence, and which, at last, we must, after all, receipt. The pence are the days; death, the receipt. For, at last, time makes known the sentence of nature's judgment upon the worth of all beings appearing in her, by destroying them:

> "And justly so; for all things, from the void
> Called forth, deserve to be destroyed;
> 'T were better, then, were nought created."
> —*Goethe.*

So, then, age and death, to which every life necessarily hurries, are the sentence of condemnation upon the will to live, passed by nature herself, which declares that this will is a striving that must frustrate itself. "What thou hast willed," it says, "ends thus; will something better." The lessons which each one learns from his life consist, on the whole, in this, that the objects of his wishes constantly delude, shake, and fall, consequently, bring more torment than pleasure, until, at length, even the whole ground and floor upon which they all stand gives way, inasmuch as his life itself is annihilated. Thus he receives the last confirmation that all his striving and willing were a blunder and error:

> Then old age and experience, hand in hand,
> Lead him to death, and make him understand,
> After a search so painful and so long,
> That all his life he has been in the wrong.

But we will enter further into the particulars of the case, since these are the views in which I have met with most opposition. First of all, I have yet to give additional evidence for the negativity of every gratification, that is, of all enjoyment and all happiness, in opposition to the positiveness of pain, by the following:

We feel pain, but not painlessness; we feel care, but not the absence of it; fear, but not security. We feel a wish as we feel hunger and thirst, but, as soon as it is satified, 'tis just as with the eaten morsel, which we feel no more the moment it is swallowed. Enjoyments and pleasures we miss painfully as soon as they fail us; but pains, even when they do not return, are not immediately missed, but are, at most, intentionally thought of by means of reflection. But only pain and want can be positively felt, and, accordingly, announce themselves; well-being, on the other hand, is merely negative. For that very reason, we do not become aware of the three greatest boons of life — health, youth, and liberty, as such — as long as we possess them, but only after we have lost them; for they, too, are negations. That days of our life were happy, we notice not until they have given place to unhappy ones. In the ratio in which enjoyments increase, susceptibility to them decreases; the habitual is no longer felt as an enjoyment. On this very account, susceptibility to suffering increases; for the absence of the customary is painfully felt. Thus, by possession, grows the number of necessities, and hence the ability to feel pain. Hours pass away more rapidly when pleasant, and more slowly when painful; because pain, not pleasure, is the positive, whose presence is felt. In like manner, we become aware of time during *ennui*, not during diversion. Both prove that our existence is then happiest when we feel it least; whence it follows that it were better not to have it at all. Great, lively joy can absolutely be thought of only as following great distress; for to a state of lasting contentment, nothing except some pastime or gratification of vanity can be added. Therefore, all poets are compelled to bring their heroes into fearful and painful situations in order to be able to liberate them; drama and epic, accordingly, picture throughout only fighting, suffering, tormented human beings; and every novel is a raree-show, where we observe the spasms and convulsions of the agonized human heart. This æsthetic necessity, Walter Scott has naïvely laid down in the "Conclusion" to his novel, "Old Mortality." Entirely in accordance with the truth I have proved, Voltaire, so favored by nature and fortune, says, "*Le bonheur n' est qu un rêve, et la douleur est réelle;*" and adds, "*il y a quatre vingts ans que je l'éprouve. Je n'y sais autre chose que me resigner, et me dire que les mouches sont nées pour être mangées par les arraignés, et les hommes pour être divoreés par les chagrins.*" ("Happiness is but a dream, and pain is real; . . . . for eighty years I have experienced it. All I can do is to resign, and tell myself that flies are born to be eaten by spiders, and men to be consumed by sorrows.")

Before any one so confidently pronounces life a desirable good, and worthy of thanks, let him calmly compare the sum of all possible pleasures which a man can enjoy in his life with all the possible sufferings which can befall him in his life. I believe it will not be difficult to strike a balance. At bottom, however, it is entirely superfluous to dispute whether good or evil predominates in the world; for even the mere existence of evil decides the matter; since evil can never be canceled by present or future good, consequently not balanced: "*Mille piacer, non vagliono un tormento.*"—*Petrarch.* ("A thousand pleasures are not worth one torment.") For, that thousands lived in happiness and delight, would never, surely, take away the anguish and death-pang of a single one; and no more does my present well-being undo my former sufferings. Hence, even if there were a hundred times less evil in the world than is the case, nevertheless, its mere existence would be sufficient to establish a truth which may be expressed in different ways, although always somewhat indirectly, namely, that we are not to rejoice, but rather to mourn, over the existence of the world; that its non-existence is preferable to its existence; that it is something which, at bottom, ought not to be, etc. Exceedingly beautiful is Byron's expression of the matter:

> "Our life is a false nature,—'tis not in
> The harmony of things, this hard decree,
> This ineradicable taint of sin,
> This boundless Upas, this all-blasting tree,
> Whose root is earth, whose leaves and branches be
> The skies, which rain their plagues on men like dew—
> Disease, death, bondage—all the woes we see—
> And worse, the woes we see not—which throb through
> The immedicable soul, with heart-aches ever new."

If the world and life ought to be here for their own sake, and, therefore, need no justification, theoretically, and no indemnity or compensation, practically, but were here, about as Spinoza and the Spinozists of to-day represent it, as the sole manifestation of a God, who, *animi causa* or to mirror himself, proceeded thus to evolve himself, and its existence, therefore, had no need of being justified by reasons, or redeemed by consequences;—then, I say, the sufferings and plagues of life would not have to be completely canceled by the joys and well-being in it; since this, as said before, is impossible, because my present pain is never compensated for by future joys, as these fill their time like the former its time; but there would have to be no sufferings at all, and also, death ought not to be, or have no terrors for us. Only in this wise would life pay for itself.

But as our condition is far more something which had better not be, so all that surrounds us bear traces of it—as in hell everything smells of sulphur—in that everything is forever imperfect and deceptive, all pleasure has its alloy, every enjoyment is partial, every entertainment carries with it its drawback, every alleviation brings fresh trouble, every remedy for our daily and hourly need leaves us in the lurch every moment, and refuses to act, the stair upon which we tread so often breaks under us, nay, mishaps great and small are the element of our life, and we, in a word, resemble

Phineus, all whose food the harpies soiled and rendered unpalatable.*

Two remedies are applied to this: Firstly, εὐλαβεία, *i. e.*, prudence, foresight, sagacity; it is insufficient and fails utterly. Secondly, stoical equanimity, which disarms every disaster by being prepared for it, and disdaining everything: practically, it becomes cynical resignation that prefers to cast off once for all every remedy and alleviation. It makes dogs of us as it did of Diogenes in the tub. The truth of the matter is, we must be miserable, and are. Moreover, the chief source of the most serious evils that can befall man, is man himself. *Homo homini lupus* (the greatest enemy of man is man.—*Pope*). Who fixes his attention upon this, beholds the world as a hell surpassing Dante's in this that each one must be the other's devil; for which, indeed, one is better fitted than the other; better than all, however, an arch-devil appearing in the shape of a conqueror who arrays several hundred thousand men against each other and cries out to them: "Suffering and Death are your destiny: now fire upon one another with guns and cannons." And they do it. As a rule, however, injustice, extreme unfairness, severity, yea, cruelty, characterize the manner in which people treat each other: an opposite conduct is a rare exception. Hereupon, and not upon your false

---

*All that we grasp offers resistance, because it has its own will that must be subdued.

theories, rests the necessity of the state and legislation. But in all cases not within reach of the law, the regardlessness of his like peculiar to man, which arises from his boundless egotism, sometimes also from malice, immediately appears. How man deals with man, negro slavery, for instance, whose final object is sugar and coffee, shows. But we need not go so far: to enter at the age of five a woolen or other factory, and thereafter daily sit in it ten, later on twelve, finally, fourteen hours, and do the same mechanical work, is dearly buying the pleasure of breathing. But this is the fate of millions, and many other millions have an analogous fate.

The rest of us, however, trivial accidents can make completely unhappy; completely happy, nothing in the world. Whatever may be said to the contrary, the happiest moment of the happiest mortal is still the moment he falls asleep, as the unhappiest moment of the unhappiest mortal, the moment he wakes up. An indirect, but certain, proof for the fact that people feel, consequently, are unhappy, is furnished overabundantly, by the intense envy dwelling in all, which is roused in all relations of life by every advantage whatever it may be and which cannot hold back its poison. Because they feel unhappy, they cannot bear the sight of a supposed happy one: he that feels happy for a moment, will at once desire to make all about him happy, and says:

Que tout le monde ici soit heureux de ma joie. (May every one be happy with me.)

If life in itself were a valuable possession and decidedly preferable to non-existence, the gate need not be occupied by such terrible guards as death and its terrors. But who would persevere in life as it is, if death were less frightful? And who could even so much as endure the thought of death, if life were a joy? However, death carries with it still the good of being the end of life, and we console ourselves about the sufferings of life with death and about death with the sufferings of life. The truth is that both belong inseparably together, forming a coil of error, a return from which is as difficult as it is desirable.

If the world were not something, which, *practically* expressed, ought not to be, it would also not be a problem, *theoretically:* much rather, its existence would either need no explanation at all, it being so self-evident that astonishment or questions about it could arise in no mind, or its object would be unmistakable. Instead of this, however, it is an insolvable problem, as the most perfect philosophy will always contain an unexplained element, like an insolvable precipitation or the remainder which the irrational ratio of two quantities always leaves. Therefore, when one dares put the question, why not, rather than this world there were nothing, the world does not justify itself; no reason, no final cause can be found in it, nor can it be proved that it is here for its own sake, that is, for its own advantage. In accordance with my doctrine, this, of course, is to be explained from the fact that the principal of its existence is expressly a groundless one, namely, blind will to live, which, being the thing *per se*, cannot be subject to the principle of sufficient reason, which is merely the form of appearances, and by which alone each why is justified. This agrees with the constitution of the world: for only a blind, not a seeing, will could have placed itself in the position in which we find ourselves. A seeing will would quite soon have made the estimate that the business does not cover expenses, since so powerful a struggling and striving, with the exertion of all powers by continual care, anguish, and want, and with the inevitable destruction of every individual life, find no indemnity in the existence thus gained, so ephemeral and coming to nought. For this very reason, the explanation of the world from an Anaxagorean νους, that is, from a will guided by *cognition*, necessarily, for its palliation, demands optimism, which, afterward, in spite of the loud testimony of a whole world full of misery, is set up and defended. Life is then proclaimed a gift, while it is clear as day, that if each one could have previously inspected and tried the gift, he would most respectfully have declined its acceptance. Lessing admired the understanding of his son, who, because he had not the least desire to enter the world, had to be drawn into it with forceps, but scarcely entered, absconded in haste. In answer to this, it is sometimes said that life, from beginning to end, is intended to be a lesson; to which every one could reply: "On that very account I would I had been left in the quiet of all-sufficient nought, where I needed neither lessons, nor anything else." Add to this that he must some day give account of every hour of his life, he is much more entitled to demand reasons for having been removed from that quiet into so dubious, dark, agonizing, and painful a position. To this, then, do false fundamental views lead us. For human existence, far from possessing the character of a *gift*, has altogether that of a contracted *debt*, whose collection appears in the shape of the pressing necessities, tormenting wishes, and endless distresses caused by that existence. To the payment of this debt, as a rule, the whole life-time is devoted; but thereby only the interest is paid; death pays the principal.—And when was this debt contracted? In generation.

Accordingly, if we look at man as a being whose existence is a punishment and an atonement, we view him in a truer light. The myth of the fall of man (although, probably, as all Judaism, taken from the Zend-Avesta: Bun-Dehesch, 15), is the only one in the Old Testament to which I can concede a metaphysical, though merely allegorical, truth; indeed, it is the only one that reconciles me to the Old Testament. To nothing else does our existence bear such a great resemblance as to the result of a false step, a punishable desire. New

Testament Christianity, whose ethical spirit is that of Brahmanism and Buddhism, therefore very foreign to the otherwise optimistic spirit of the Old Testament, has, very wisely, directly begun with that mythus: indeed, without this, it would not have found a point of attachment at all in Judaism. If one wishes to estimate the degree of guilt with which our existence itself is infected, behold the suffering inseparable from it. Every great pain, be it physical or mental, shows clearly what we deserve: for we would not suffer, if we did not deserve it. That also Christianity views our existence in this light, is testified by a passage from Luther's Commentaries on the Galatians, Ch. 3, which I have only in Latin: "*Sumus autem nos omnes corporibus et rebus subjecti Diabolo, et hospites sumus in mundo, cujus ipse princeps et Deus est. Ideo panis, quem edimus, potus quem bibimus, vestes, quibus utimur, imo aër et totum quo vivimus in carne, sub ipsius imperio est.*" ("All of us, moreover, in body and possessions, are subject to the Devil, and we are sojourners in a world of which he himself is chief and lord. So the bread we eat, the water we drink, the clothes we wear, nay, even the air and all which gives us sustenance is under his sway.") They have cried out against the melancholy and disconsolateness of my philosophy; it lies, however, only in this, that I, instead of fabling a future hell as an equivalent for sin, proved that, where guilt exists in the world, there is already something resembling hell; who denies this, may some day experience it himself.

And to this world, this arena of tormented and agonized beings, who subsist only by devouring one another, where, therefore, every wild beast is the living grave of a thousand others, and its self-preservation a series of deaths by torture; where, with cognition, the susceptibility to pain increases, which, on that account, reaches its highest degree in man, and a higher degree in proportion to his intelligence,— to this world they have attempted to adapt the system of *optimism*, and to demonstrate it as the best of all possible worlds. How glaring the absurdity! However, an optimist bids me open my eyes and gaze upon the world, so beautiful in the sunlight, with its mountains, valleys, streams, plants, and animals. But, then, is the world a panorama? These things, of course, are beautiful to *behold;* but to *be* one of them is altogether different. Then comes a teleologist and praises the wise arrangement which provides that the planets do not rush together; land and sea are not reduced to a pulp, but kept nicely apart; all is not benumbed by continual frost nor roasted by heat; likewise, in consequence of the obliquity of the ecliptic, there is no eternal spring, since thus nothing could come to maturity. But these and all similar things are simply *conditiones sine quibus non*. If there is to be a world at all, if its planets are to exist at least long enough for a ray of light from a remote fixed star to reach them, and not, like Lessing's son, scud off immediately after birth,— then, of course, it durst not be framed so unskilfully that the very scaffolding threatened to collapse. But if one proceeds to the *results* of that lauded work, contemplates the *players* who act upon the so durably framed stage, and *then* sees that with sensibility pain sets in and increases in proportion to the intelligence, that then, keeping pace with this, lust and suffering become more and more prominent, until, at last, human life offers no other material than for tragedies and comedies, then, who does not play the hypocrite, will hardly be disposed to sing hallelujahs. The real, but concealed, origin of the latter has, moreover, been unsparingly, but with triumphant truth, disclosed by David Hume, in his Natural History of Religion, Sects. 6, 7, 8, and 13. He also lays bare, in the tenth and eleventh books of his Dialogues on Natural Religion, with arguments very cogent, and yet very different from mine, the sad condition of this world and the untenableness of all optimism; on this occasion he also attacks the latter in its origin. Both works of Hume are as worthy of being read, as they are unknown in Germany to-day. Here, patriotically, they find incredible satisfaction in the disgusting jargon of native, ordinary minds, and proclaim them great men. Those Dialogues, however, Hamann translated, Kant revised the translation, and even in old age urged Hamann's son to publish them, because

Platner's edition was unsatisfactory. (Vide. Kant's Biography, by F. W. Schubert, p. 81–165.) From every page of David Hume there is more to be learned than from Hegel's, Herbart's, and Schleiermacher's complete philosophical works put together.

The founder of systematic *optimism* is Leibnitz, whose merits as a philosopher I do not intend to deny, although I never succeeded in thoroughly grasping the monadology, preéstablished harmony, *identitas indiscernibilium.* His *Nouveaux Essais sur l' entendement*, however, are merely an excerpt from Locke, with a detailed, but weak critique, intended to correct his justly world-renowned work, which he here opposes with as little success as he opposes Newton by his *Tentamen de motuum coelestium causis,* directed against his theory of gravitation. Against this Leibnitz-Wolfian philosophy, the Critique of Pure Reason is especially directed, and stands to it in a polemic, nay, annihilating relation; as to Locke and Hume, in one of continuation and development. That, at the present day, professors of philosophy are everywhere anxious to set Leibnitz with his blunders on his feet again, yes, to glorify him, and to esteem Kant as little as possible, has its good reasons in the *primum vivere.* The Critique of Pure Reason, namely, does not allow one to give out Jewish mythology for philosophy, or to talk familiarly of the soul as of a given reality or a well known and well accredited person, without giving account of how one came to this idea, and what authority one has to use it scientifically. But *primum vivere, deinde philosophari!* Down with Kant, *vivat* our Leibnitz! But to return to this one, I can concede no other merit to the Theodicy, this methodical and broad unfolding of optimism, as such, than that of having given rise, afterward, to the immortal *Candide* of the great Voltaire, in which, indeed, the oft-repeated, lame excuse of Leibnitz for the evils of the world, namely, that bad sometimes leads to good, found an unexpected support. By the very name of his hero, Voltaire indicated that uprightness alone was necessary to recognize the opposite of optimism. Truly, on this theatre of sin, of suffering, and of death, optimism cuts such a strange figure, that it would seem to be irony, had we not a sufficient explanation of its origin, in its secret source, so amusingly disclosed by Hume, as above mentioned (namely, feigning flattery, with insulting confidence in its success).

To the palpably sophistical proofs of Leibnitz, that this is the best of all possible worlds, the proof that it is the *worst* of all possible worlds, may seriously and honestly be opposed. For possible does not mean what one may idly fancy, but what can really exist and endure. Now, this world is so constituted as it had to be in order to barely exist. Consequently, a worse world, since it could not exist, is not possible at all; this very one, therefore, is the worst possible. For, not only if the planets should collide, but also, if of the really occurring perturbations of their course, anyone, instead of gradually adjusting itself by another, should continue to augment, the world would soon come to an end. Astronomers know upon how accidental circumstances, namely, mostly upon the irrational relation of the periods of rotation, this depends, and have laboriously figured out that it may all end well; hence, the world can just about maintain its place. We hope, although Newton was of an opposite opinion, that they have not made a mistake, and therefore the mechanical *perpetuum mobile*, realized in such a planetary system, do not, like the others, cease to move. Under the firm rind of the planet rage the mighty forces of nature, which, as soon as an accident gives them free play, must destroy it with all living beings. This has occurred to our planet at least three times, and may frequently happen again: An earthquake of Lisbon, of Hayti, a destruction of Pompeii, are merely petty allusions to the possibility. A trifling change in the atmosphere, chemically not even noticeable, causes cholera, yellow-fever, blackdeath and the like, which carry off millions; any greater change would extinguish all life. A very moderate rise in the temperature would dry up all the rivers and springs. Animals have been endowed with organs and powers barely enough to suffice for providing themselves with the means of subsistence and for rearing their young; so that when an animal loses a limb, or only the complete use of it, it must in most cases die. Even of the human race, however powerful tools it may have in the shape of understanding and reason, nine-tenths live in continual battle with want, forever on the verge of destruction, maintaining themselves above it with difficulty and exertion. So, throughout, to the continuance of the whole as well as to that of each individual, the conditions are given niggardly and meagerly, but nothing more. Therefore, individual life passes in an incessant struggle for existence; while at every step destruction threatens. Just because this threat is so often executed, provision had to be made by means of the incredibly great surplus of germs, that the destruction of the individuals might not lead to that of the *genera*, in which alone nature takes serious interest. The world is consequently as bad as it possibly can be and exist at all. *q. e. d.* The petrifaction of the entirely different *genera* of animals formerly inhabiting the planet, furnish as verification the documents of worlds whose existence was no longer possible. These, consequently, were somewhat worse than the worst of all possible worlds.

Optimism is at the bottom the unwarrantable self-praise of the true originator of the world, the will to live, which complacently mirrors itself in its work; accordingly, it is not only a false, but also a pernicious, doctrine. For it represents life as a desirable state, and, as its object, the happiness of man. With this in view, each one then believes he has the justest claim to fortune and enjoyment; but if, as usually happens, these do not fall to his lot, he believes that he is wronged, nay, that he misses the object of his existence; while it is much more correct to consider (as Brahmanism and Buddhism, and also genuine Christianity do), as the object of our life, work, privation, distress, and suffering, crowned by death; because these lead to the denial of the will to live. In the New Testament the world is represented as a vale of tears, life as a purifying process, and an instrument of torture is the symbol of Christianity. Accordingly, when Leibnitz, Shaftesbury, Bolingbroke, and Pope stepped forward with optimism, the offense generally taken was that optimism was incompatible with Christianity; this, Voltaire, in the preface to his excellent poem, "*Le désastre de Lisbonne,*" which likewise is expressly directed against optimism, relates and explains. What puts this great man, whom I, in opposition to the revilings of venal German scribblers, so gladly praise, decidedly above Rousseau, inasmuch as it testifies the greater depth of his thought, is his insight into three truths: 1. The great preponderance of evil and wretchedness, by which he is deeply permeated; 2. The strict necessitation of the acts of the will; 3. Locke's principle, that possibly the thinking faculty may also be material; while Rousseau contests all this, by declamations in his "*Profession de foi du vicaire*

Savoyard," a flat, Protestant parson-philosophy. He also, in the same spirit, combats the just-mentioned beautiful poem of Voltaire with a perverted, shallow, and logically false ratiocination in favor of optimism, in his long letter to Voltaire of the 18th of August, 1756, devoted to this special purpose. Indeed, the fundamental trait and grand mistake of Rosseau's whole philosophy is, that in place of the Christian doctrine of hereditary sin and the original depravity of the human race, he assumes an original goodness and unlimited perfectibility, which has gone astray only with civilization and its consequences. Upon this he founds his optimism and humanism.

As Voltaire, in the *Candide*, wages war in his playful manner with optimism, so does Byron, in his immortal masterpiece, *Cain*, in his serious and tragic manner. For this, he has been glorified by the invectives of the obscurantist Frederick Schlegel. Finally, in order to corroborate my view, were I to cite the sayings of all the great minds of all times who were opposed to optimism, there would be no end of quotations, as almost every one of them has expressed his recognition of the wretchedness of this world in strong terms. Therefore, not to confirm, but merely to adorn, this chapter, a few expressions of this sort may find room at the end.

First of all, it may be mentioned that the Greeks, strangers as they were to the Christian and Upper

Asiatic views of the world, and took decidedly the standpoint of affirming the will to live, were deeply impressed with the misery of existence. This is testified by the invention of tragedy, which is due to them. Another voucher is furnished by the custom of the Thracians to welcome the newly-born with lamentations, and to mention all the evils which he was to encounter; on the contrary, to bury the dead with joy and jests, because he was at last free from so many great sufferings; which reads thus in a beautiful verse preserved by Plutarch (*De audiend. poet. in fine*):

> Τον φυντα ϑρηνειν, εις οσ' ερχεται κακα.
> Τον δ'αυ ϑανοντα και πονων πεπαυμενον
> Χαιροντας ευφημουντας εκπεμπειν δομων.

> "They mourned the new-born child of earth,
>   Embarking on life's stormy sea;
> But hailed its death with joy and mirth,
>   Releasing it from misery."

Not to any historical connection, but to the moral identity of the matter, is it to be attributed, that the Mexicans welcomed the newly-born with the words: "My child, thou art born to endure: therefore, endure, suffer, and be silent." And following the same feeling, Swift (as Walter Scott relates in his life) had early adopted the habit of keeping his birthday as a time, not of joy, but of sadness, and of reading on that day that passage in the Bible in which Job mourns over and curses the day when it was said in his father's house: "A son is born."

Well known, and too long to copy, is the passage in the Apology of Socrates, where Plato makes this wisest of mortals say that death, even if it robbed us forever of consciousness, would be a wonderful gain, since a deep, dreamless sleep were preferable to any day, even of the happiest life.

A saying of Heraklitos runs thus:

Τῳ ουν βιῳ ονομα μεν βιος, εργον δε θανατος.

"Life ideed, we call life; in reality, it is death."

Famous is the beautiful stanza of Theognis:

Αρχην μεν μη φυναι επιχθονιοιδιν αριστον,
Μηδ' εισιδειν αυγας οξεος ηελιου
Φυντα δ' οπως ωκιστα πυλας Αἴδαο περησαι,
Και κεισθαι πολλην γην επαμησαμενον.

"Not to be born — never to see the sun —
No worldly blessing is a greater one!
And the next best is speedily to die,
And lapt beneath a load of earth to lie!"

Sophocles in the *Oedipus Colonos* (1225), abbreviates this thus:

Μη φυναι τον απαντα νι-
Κᾳ λογον το δ'επει φανῃ,
βηναι κεισθεν, οθεν περ ηκει,
Πολυ δευτερον, ὡς ταχιστα.

"Not to have been born at all is superior to every view of the question; and this, when one may have seen the light, to return thence, whence he came, as quickly as possible, is far the next best."

Euripides says:

> Πας δ'οδυνηρος βιος ανθρωπων,
> Κ'ουκ εστι πονων αναπαυσις.
>
> "But the whole life of man is full of grief,
> Nor is there rest from toils."

Even Homer has said it:

> "For ah! what is there of inferior birth
> That breathes or creeps upon the dust of earth,
> What wretched creature, of what wretched kind,
> Than man, more weak, calamitous, and blind?"

Pliny says: *Quapropter hoc primum quisque in remediis animi sui habeat, ex omnibus bonis, quae homini natura tribuit, nullum melius esse tempestiva morte—* (*Hist. Nat.*, 28, 2). "Let each then reckon this as one great solace to his mind, that of all the blessings which nature has bestowed on man, there is none greater than the death which comes at a seasonable hour.

Shakespeare puts these words into the mouth of the aged King Henry IV.:

> "O heaven! That one might read the book of fate,
> And see the revolution of the times,
> .   .   .   .   .   how chances mock,
> And changes fill the cup of alteration
> With divers liquors! O, if this were seen,
> The happiest youth,—viewing his progress through,
> What perils past, what crosses to ensue,—
> Would shut the book and sit him down and die."

Finally, Byron:

> "Count o'er the joys thine hours have seen,
> Count o'er thy days from anguish free,
> And know, whatever thou hast been,
> 'Tis something better not to be."

Baltazar Gracian, too, depicts the misery of existence in the blackest colors in the *Criticon*, *Parte* 1, *Crisi* 5, at the beginning, and *Crisi* 7, at the end, where he fully represents life as a tragic farce.

No one, however, has treated the subject so thoroughly and exhaustively as Leopardi, in our own days. He is wholly filled and permeated with it; everywhere the mockery and misery of this existence are his theme; on every page of his works he represents them, but with such diversity of form and expression, with such wealth of illustration, that he never wearies, but rather entertains and stimulates us throughout.

THE METAPHYSICS OF LOVE.

> "Ihr Weisen hoch und tief gelahrt,
>   Die ihr's ersinnt und wisst,
> Wie, wo und wann sich Alles paart?
>   Warum sich's liebt und kuesst?
> Ihr hohen Weisen, sagt mir's an!
>   Ergruebelt, was mir da,
>   Ergruebelt mir, wo, wie und wann,
>   Warum mir so geschah?"—*Buerger*.

THIS chapter is the last of four, whose manifold, mutual relation, by virtue of which they form, to a certain extent, a subordinate whole, the attentive reader will recognize, without my being compelled to interrupt my discourse by appeals and references.

Poets we are wont to see engaged chiefly in depicting love. As a rule, this is the principle theme of all dramatic works, be they tragic or comic, romantic or classic, Hindoo or European. Not less is it the subject-matter of by far the greater part of lyric as well as of epic poetry; especially, if we include under the latter the cart-loads of romances, which, for centuries, in all the civilized countries of Europe, every year produces as regularly as the fruits of the soil. All these works are substantially nothing but many-sided, brief or detailed, descriptions of this passion. Likewise, the most successful delineations of it, as, for instance, Romeo and Juliet, The New Heloise, Werther, have achieved immortal glory. If, notwithstanding, Rochefoucauld supposes that it were with passionate love as with ghosts, all spoke of them, but none ever saw them, and also Lichtenberg, in his essay "On the Power of Love," contests and denies the reality and naturalness of that passion: it is a great error. For it is impossible that something foreign to and contradicting human nature, consequently, a mere imaginary caricature, could, at all times, be indefatigably represented by poetic genius and received by humanity with unchanged interest; for without truth there can be nothing beautiful in art:

"*Rien n'est beau que le vrai; le vrai seul est aimable.*"

"Nought is fair save the true; the true alone is lovely."

Indeed, experience, though not the daily, confirms that that which, as a rule, occurs but as a lively, still superable inclination, can, under certain circumstances, increase to a passion surpassing all others in violence, then doing away with all considerations, overcoming all hindrances with incredible strength and perseverance, so that for its indulgence life is unhesitatingly risked, nay, if such should absolutely be denied, even sacrificed. The Werthers and Jacopo Ortises exist not in romances only, but every year there are to be found at least half a dozen of them in Europe; *sed ignotis perierunt mortibus illi:* for their sufferings find no chronicler but the writer of official records or the reporter. Yet the readers of the police records in English and French daily papers will testify to the correctness of my assertion. Greater still is the number of those whom the same passion brings into the mad-house. Finally, each year can show up here and there a case of mutual suicide, where the loving couple have been hindered by external circumstances. However, I cannot understand why those who are assured of mutual love, and expect to find the highest bliss in its enjoyment, do not rather take the extremest steps and withdraw from all relations, instead of giving up with life a happiness than which they can conceive of no greater. But as far as the lower degrees and mere touches of that passion are concerned, we all have them daily before our eyes, and in our hearts, too, as long as we are not old.

Accordingly, after what has been here recalled to mind, one cannot question either the reality or the importance of the subject. Therefore, instead of wondering that even a philosopher now makes this constant theme of all poets his own, one ought rather to wonder that a matter which plays such an important part throughout human life, has been hitherto scarcely at all taken into consideration by philosophers, and lies before us as raw material. More than all others, Plato, particularly in the Symposium and Phaedrus, has dealt with it; however, what he states is within the range of myths, fables, and jests, and concerns, for the most part, Grecian boy-love. The little that Rousseau, in the "*Discours sur l' inégalité* (*p.* 96, *ed. Bip.*), says upon our theme is wrong and insufficient. Kant's discussion of the subject, in the third chapter of the dissertation "On the Feeling of the Beautiful and the Sublime," is very superficial, and shows a lack of experience, and, therefore, is partly incorrect. Finally, Platner's treatment of the subject, in his Anthropology, every one will find flat and shallow. Spinoza's definition, however, on account of its wonderful *naiveté*, deserves to be quoted for the reader's exhilaration: "*Amor est titillatio, concomitante idea causae externae.*" (*Eth. IV., prop.* 44, *dem.*) "Love is a tickling, with the concomitant idea of an external cause." Predecessors, accordingly, I have neither to take advantage of nor to refute: the matter has forced itself upon me objectively, and entered, of its own accord, into the chain of my speculations. Moreover, I can hope for least applause from those who are at the time swayed by this passion, and, accordingly, seek to express their overpowering feelings in the sublimest and most ethereal images; my view will seem too physical, too material, to them; metaphysical, nay, transcendent, as it is in reality. May they previously consider that the being who to-day inspires them to madrigals and sonnets, had she been born eighteen years earlier, would win scarcely a glance from them.

For all love, ethereally as it may demean itself, roots in sexual instinct alone, nay, is absolutely only a more closely defined, specialized, perhaps, even, in the strictest sense, individualized sexual instinct. If now, keeping this in view, we contemplate the important part which love, in all its gradations and shades, plays, not only in dramas and romances, but also in the real world, where it, next to love of life, proves the strongest and most active of all incentives; continually engages half the powers and thoughts of the younger portion of humanity; is the last goal of almost every human endeavor; gains influence over the most important affairs; interrupts at every hour the most serious occupations; unbalances at times even the greatest minds; does not hesitate to enter importunely with its trash into the transactions of statesmen and the researches of scholars; knows how to put its loveletters and ringlets of hair even into ministerial port-folios and philosophical manuscripts; no less, daily contrives the saddest and most complicated quarrels; dissolves the most important relations; sunders the strongest ties; sacrifices sometimes life or health, sometimes wealth, rank, and happiness, nay, makes unscrupulous the otherwise honest; the hitherto faithful, treacherous; accordingly, appears as a malevolent demon who is anxious to pervert, confuse, and overthrow all;—then we are prone to exclaim: to what end this noise? to what end this driving, raging, anxiety, and distress? Nothing is at stake but that every Jack may find his Jill;* why should such a trifle play so important a part, and unceasingly bring disturbance and confusion into the well-regulated affairs of life?

But to the earnest searcher the spirit of truth gradually discloses the answer; it is no trifle which is at stake; on the contrary, the importance of the matter is fully adequate to the earnestness and ardor of this turmoil. The final purpose of all love intrigues, be they played in sock or buskin, is really more important than all the other aims of human life, and, therefore, fully worth the deep earnestness with which it is prosecuted. In fact, what is decided thereby is really nothing less than the *character of the next generation*. The *dramatis personæ* who will appear when we have departed, are here, as regards their existence and constitution, determined by these frivolous love-affairs. As the *existence* (their existing at all) of those future persons is throughout conditioned by our sexual instinct in general, so their *essence* (what they are) is conditioned by individual selection in its gratification,

---

*I dare not fully express myself here: the gentle reader must therefore translate the phrase into Aristophanic language.

that is, by love, and thereby, in every respect, irrevocably established. This is the key to the problem. In applying the key, we will learn to know it better, if we review the degrees of love, from the most fleeting inclination to the most powerful passion. We shall see that the difference arises from the degree of individualization in the selection.

All the *love-affairs* of the present generation put together are, accordingly, mankind's serious *meditatio compositionis generationis futurae, e qua iterum pendent innumerae generationes.* In this matter, not as in every other, is *individual* weal and woe at stake, but the existence and special constitution of the whole race in time to come. Accordingly, the will of the individual appears in a higher degree as the will of the *genus.* Upon this importance rest the pathetic and sublime of love-affairs, the transcendent of its raptures and griefs, which poets, for thousands of years, have not wearied of picturing, since no theme can vie with this in interest; for it concerns the weal and woe of the *genus*, and stands to all others, which concern only the weal and woe of the individual, in the relation of body to surface. On this very account, it is so difficult to impart interest to a drama without love-affairs, and, otherwise, this theme is never exhausted, not even by daily use.

That which in the individual consciousness manifests itself as sexual instinct in general, and without concentration upon a definite individual of the opposite sex, is *per se* and outside of the appearance purely the will to live. But that which appears in the consciousness as sexual instinct directed towards a particular individual, is *per se* the will to live as a certain definite individual. In this case, sexual instinct, though *per se* a subjective desire, knows very skillfully how to adopt the mask of an objective admiration and so deceive the consciousness. For nature needs this strategem for her purposes. That in every case of love, however objective and of sublime a tinge as that admiration may appear, nothing but the generation of an individual of a certain, definite constitution is intended, is, in the first place, confirmed by this, that not returned love but possession, that is, physical enjoyment is the essential. Assurance of the former, therefore, is in no wise a consolation for the want of the latter; in such an extremity, indeed, many a one has shot himself. On the other hand, those deep in love are content with possession, that is, physical enjoyment, if they cannot obtain a return of love. For this, all forced marriages, as well as the favor of a woman, often bought, in spite of her aversion, with great presents or other sacrifices, nay, even cases of rape, vouch. That this particular child be born, is the true object of the whole love-romance, though unknown to the participants. The way and manner in which it is reached, is of secondary importance. Loudly as the lofty and sentimental, and especially the enamored souls may here cry out against the stern realism of my view, they are, nevertheless, wrong. For is not the exact determination of the individualities of the next generation a much higher and worthier object than their overpowering feelings and supersensual soap-bubbles? Nay, can there be an earthly aim greater or more important? It alone is adequate to the depth with which passionate love is felt, to the earnestness with which it appears, and to the importance which it attributes even to the trifles within its reach. Only by assuming this object as the true one, do the prolixities, the endless troubles and torments to obtain the beloved object seem commensurate to the matter. For it is the coming generation, in its entire individual determination, which, by means of that turmoil and anxiety, presses on into existence. Yes, it stirs even in the circumspective, determined, and capricious selection to gratify the sexual intinct, which is called love. The growing affection of two lovers is really already the life-will of the new individual whom they can and would like to beget; nay, even in the meeting of their yearning glances, his new life is kindled and manifests itself as a future, harmonious, well-organized individual: they feel a longing for a real union and amalgamation into a single being, to henceforth continue to live only in this one. This is fulfilled in the offspring, in whom the qualities inherited from both, amalgamated and united, are perpetuated. Conversely, the mutual, decided, and constant aversion between a man and maiden is an indication that what they could beget would be an ill-organized, unharmonious, unhappy being. Therefore, there is a deep meaning in Calderon's calling the atrocious Semiramis the daughter of the air, but introducing her as the child of rape, after which follows the murder of the husband.

But, finally, what draws two individuals of opposite sex with such violence towards one another is the will to live representing itself in the whole *genus*, which here anticipates an objectivation of its being, corresponding to its purposes, in the individual which the two can beget. This individual inherits from the father the will or character; from the mother, the intellect; the physique, from both; though, generally, the shape takes after the father, the size, after the mother,—in accordance with the law which is revealed in hybrids. Inexplicable as is each ones distinctive individuality, and exclusively peculiar as it is to him, so is also the peculiar and individual passion of two lovers,—yes, ultimately, both are one and the same thing. The former implies what is realized in the latter. As the very first origin of a new individual and true *punctum saliens* of its life must really be considered the moment that the parents begin to love one another;—to fancy each other, is a very striking English expression,—and, as said before, in the meeting and fixing of their yearning glances arises the first germ of a new being, who, indeed, like most germs, is usually crushed. This new individual is, to a certain extent, a new Platonic idea; now, as all ideas strive with the greatest vehemence to become visible, seizing with desire the matter which the law of causality distributes among them, so, too, this special idea of a human individuality strives, with the greatest desire and violence, for its realization in an appearance. This desire and violence is, in fact, the passion of the future parents for one another. There are innumerable degrees of it, whose extremes, may, if you will, be devoted as Αφροδιτη πανδημος and ουρανια, yet it is, essentially, the same everywhere. Moreover, according to the degree, it will be the more powerful the more individualized it is; that is, the more the beloved individual, by virtue of all her parts and qualities, is exclusively fit to satisfy the wish and needs of the lover, which are determined by her own individuality. But what is here at stake will become clear to us further on. Primarily and essentially, amorous inclination is directed toward health, strength, and beauty, consequently, towards youth; because the will desires to represent, first of all, the generic character, this being the basis of all individuality, of the human species; every-day flirtation, Αφροδιτη πανδημος, does not go much beyond this. With this are connected more special demands, which we later will examine more particularly, and with which, where they forsee satisfaction, passion increases. The highest degrees of this passion, however, arise from that fitness of both individualities for one another, by virtue of which the will, that is the character, of the father and the intellect of the mother, in their union, just complete that individual for which the will in general, which represents itself in the whole *genus*, feels a yearning commensurate with its own greatness, therefore transcending the measure of a mortal heart,—a yearning whose motives lie beyond the reach of the individual intellect. This, then, is the soul of a real, great passion. The more complete the mutual fitness of the individuals in each of the manifold respects to be considered, the stronger will their mutual passion prove. Since there are no two persons exactly alike, to each particular man a particular woman must correspond most completely,—always with regard to the future child. Rare as the accident of their meeting is real, passionate love. However, the possibility of it being ever present in all, its representation in the works of the poets is intelligible to us. Just because the passion of love is properly concerned with the offspring and his qualities, and here its nucleus lies, there can be friendship between two young and well-educated persons of opposite sex by virtue of the harmony of their disposition, character, and mental proclivities, without sexual love interfering. Nay, in this respect there can exist between them even a certain aversion. The reason for this is, that the child would, physically or mentally, have unharmonious qualities; in short, his existence and constitution would not be adequate to the purposes of the will to live as represented in the *genus*. In the opposite case, with heterogeneity of disposition, of character, and of mental inclination, and with the aversion, nay, animosity, resulting therefrom, love can still arise and exist; where it then blinds them to all, so that, if it misleads them to marriage, it becomes a very unhappy one.

But now to a more thorough examination of the matter. Egoism is such a deep-rooted property of all individuality that, to arouse the activity of an individual being, only egoistic motives can be relied upon with safety. To be sure, the *genus* has an earlier, nearer, and greater right to the individual, than the perishable individuality itself; nevertheless, when the individual ought to be active, and even offer sacrifice for the continuance and constitution of the *genus*, the importance of the matter cannot be made so clear to his intellect, which is intended merely for individual purposes, that he would act in accordance with it. Therefore, in such a case, nature can gain her purpose only by implanting in the individual a certain illusion, through which that appears as a benefit to himself, which is, in truth, one for the *genus* only; so that he serves the latter while supposing that he serves himself. In this process, a mere chimera, immediately disappearing, floats before him, and as a motive takes the place of a reality. This *illusion* is *instinct*. In most cases, it may be looked upon as the sense of the *genus*, which represents to the will whatever subserves it. But because the will has here become individual, he must be deceived in such a manner that he may behold through sense of the *individual* what the sense of the *genus* presents him; that is, fancy to prosecute individual, while, in truth, he prosecutes generic, aims — this word here taken in its full sense. The external appearance of instinct we observe best in animals, where the part it plays is most significant; but the internal process we can, like everything internal, learn to know only in ourselves. However, it is supposed that man has scarcely any instinct, or, at all events, only that of seeking and taking, when a babe, the mother's breast. But, in fact, we have a very definite, distinct, even complex, instinct, namely, the fine, earnest, and capricious selection of the other individual. With this gratification, as such, that is, so far as it is a sensual enjoyment, resting upon an urgent necessity of the individual, the beauty or ugliness of the other person has nothing whatever to do. The regard for this, so zealously pursued, together with the careful selection arising therefrom, evidently does not refer to the chooser himself, although he supposes it to be the case, but to the true object,— the offspring,— in whom the type of the *genus* is to be preserved as genuine and correct as possible. By a thousand physical accidents and moral repugnances, there arise many kinds of degeneration of the human form; nevertheless, the genuine type is, in all its parts, restored; which is brought about under the guidance of the sense of beauty, that throughout leads the sexual instinct, and without which this would sink into a repulsive want. Accordingly, every one, in the first place, will decidedly prefer, and eagerly desire, the most beautiful persons, that is, such in whom the character of the *genus* is most purely expressed; secondly, he will demand from the other individual especially those perfections which he himself lacks; yes, even find beautiful those imperfections that are opposed to his own. Therefore, small men seek large women; blondes love brunettes, etc. The giddy rapture which seizes a man at the sight of a woman of beauty suited to him, and pictures to him a union with her as the highest good, is that very *sense of the genus*, which, recognizing its clearly expressed stamp, would like to perpetuate the *genus* with this stamp. Upon this decided inclination for beauty rests the preservation of the type of the genus: therefore, it acts so forcibly. We will, farther on, treat the consideration which it follows. What here leads man, is really an instinct which is intended for the best of the *genus*, while man imagines that he is seeking only his own greater enjoyment. In fact, we here have an instructive revelation of the inner essence of *all* instinct, which, throughout, as in this instance, puts the individual to work for the good of the *genus*. For manifestly the care with which an insect seeks a certain flower, or fruit, or dung, or flesh, or, as the ichneumon seeks a strange insect-larva to lay its eggs *there*, and, to attain this, heeds neither toil nor danger, is very analogous to the care with which a man selects for sexual gratification a woman of definite character, adapted to him, and so eagerly strives to possess her, that often, in order to reach this end, he sacrifices, in spite of all reasons, his life's happiness by a foolish marriage, by love intrigues which cost him fortune, honor, and life, even by crimes, as adultery or rape, and all merely in order to serve, in accordance with the everywhere sovereign will of nature, the *genus* in the most efficient manner, though at the expense of the individual. Everywhere instinct is working as though with a purpose, and yet entirely without one. Nature implants it, when the acting individual would be incapable of understanding or unwilling to prosecute the object: therefore, it is, as a rule, given only to beasts, and especially to the lowest, who have least understanding; but almost only in the case here considered, also to man, who could, indeed, understand the object, but would not prosecute it with the necessary zeal, that is, even to the detriment of his own individual welfare. Thus, here as in all instinct, truth assumes the shape of illusion in order to influence the will.

A voluptuous illusion it is, deluding man, that he will find in the arms of a woman of beauty pleasing him, greater enjoyment than in those of any other; or even an illusion fixed exclusively upon a single individual, which firmly convinces him that her possession will yield him overpowering bliss. Accordingly, he imagines it is for his own enjoyment that he wastes trouble and makes sacrifices, while he does so merely to preserve the regular type of the *genus*, or even that a particular individuality, which can be born only from these parents, may come to life. So completely does the character of instinct, that is, a process as though with a purpose and yet entirely without it, here exist, that the one who is impelled by that illusion often even abhors, and would prevent the purpose, that is, generation, which alone influences him; namely, in almost all illicit amours. In accordance with the described character of the matter, after he has finally obtained satisfaction, every lover will experience a wonderful disappointment. He is amazed that what was desired so passionately accomplishes no more than any other sexual gratification. That wish stood to all his other wishes in the same relation as the *genus* stands to the individual; that is, as an infinite to a finite. The gratification, however, benefits only the *genus*, and does not, therefore, come within the consciousness of the individual, who, here inspired by the will of the *genus*, serves, with self-sacrifice of every description, a purpose not at all his own. Therefore, every lover, after the final completion of the great work, finds himself deceived: for the illusion has vanished, by means of which here the individual was the dupe of the *genus*. In accordance with this, Plato very strikingly says: ἡδονη ἁπαντων αλαζονέστατον. (*Phil.* 319).

All this, however, on its part, reflects light upon the instincts of animals. Undoubtedly, they, too, are possessed of a kind of illusion which promises them pleasure, while they work so busily and with self-denial for the *genus*. The bird builds its nest; the insect seeks a fitting place for its eggs, or even hunts for prey, which, unpalatable to itself, must be laid with the eggs as food for the future *larvæ*. The bee, the wasp, the ant, apply themselves to their artificial structures and to their highly complex economy. All of them are certainly guided by an illusion which conceals the service of the *genus* under the mask of an egoistic motive. This is probably the only way of making comprehensible to ourselves the *inner* or subjective process which lies at the bottom of the manifestations of instinct. Outwardly, however, or objectively, we find, in animals strongly swayed by instinct, a preponderance of the ganglionic, or *subjective* nervous system over the *objective*, or cerebral system. From this may be concluded that they are impelled, not so much by an objective, proper apprehension, as by subjective representations, which arouse desire, that arise through the influence of the ganglionic system upon the brain. Hence, they are influenced by a certain *illusion*. This seems to be the *physiological* process in all instinct. As a farther illustration, I may mention as another, though weaker, example of instinct, the capricious appetite of those *enceinte*. It seems to arise from the fact that the nourishment of the embryo demands, at times, a peculiar and definite modification of the blood flowing to it; whereupon the food that is to effect such a modification, at once represents itself to the mother as an object of strong desire, so that an illusion arises. Accordingly, woman has one instinct more than man. The ganglionic system, too, is more developed in woman. From the great excess of brain in man, it is to be explained that he has fewer instincts than animals have, and that even those few can easily be misled. Namely, the sense of beauty, instinctively guiding the selection for sexual gratification, is misled when it degenerates into a propensity to pederasty. Analogous to this, the flesh-fly, *musca vomitoria*, instead of depositing her eggs, as her instinct prompts her, into decomposing meat, lays them into the blossom of *arum dracunculus*, misled by the decaying odor of this plant. That an instinct wholly concerned with the offspring lies at the bottom of all love, will gain entire certainty by a more minute analysis, from which, therefore, we cannot withdraw. First of all, it must be mentioned that, by nature, man is inclined to inconstancy, woman, to constancy, in love. A man's love sinks noticeably the moment it is satisfied. Almost every other woman moves him more than the one he possesses: he longs for a change. A woman's love, on the contrary, increases from that very moment. This is the consequence of the purpose of nature, who intends to preserve and, therefore, increase the *genus* as much as possible. For a man can conveniently beget more than a hundred children in a year, if as many women were at his disposal; a woman, however, with never so many men, could bear but *one* child in a year (omitting twin-births). Therefore, *he* always looks for other women; *she*, however, clings to the one she has: for nature impels her to preserve, instinctively and without reflection, the provider and defender of the future brood. Accordingly, conjugal fidelity is artificial to man, natural to woman; and so, woman's adultery, objectively, on account of the consequences, as well as subjectively, on account of its unnaturalness, is far more unpardonable than man's. But to be thorough, and gain the full conviction that the delight in the other sex, objective as it may appear to us, is merely masked instinct, that is, the sense of the *genus* striving to preserve its type, we must even examine more closely the considerations which guide us in this pleasure, and enter into particulars, strange as the latter may figure in a philosophical work. These considerations are divided into those which concern immediately the type of the *genus*, that is, beauty; into those which concern physical qualities; and lastly, into those merely relative, which arise from the necessary and mutual correction and neutralization of the one-sidedness and abnormities of the two individuals. We will examine them singly.

The primary consideration guiding our choice and inclination is the *age*. On the whole, it is effective from the years of beginning to those of ending menstruation. However, we give decided preference to the period from the eighteenth to the twenty-eighth year. Outside of those years, no woman can excite us; an old woman arouses our disgust. Youth without beauty, still has its charm; beauty without youth, none. Manifestly the purpose here unconsciously guiding us is the possibility of generation itself: therefore, all persons lose in charm for the other sex in the measure in which they depart from the period best adapted to generation or conception. The second consideration is *health*. Acute diseases disturb only temporarily; chronic diseases, or even cachexy, repel, because the child inherits them. The third consideration is the *skeleton*, because it is the basis of the type of the *genus*. Next to old age and disease, nothing so repels us as a deformed figure; even the most beautiful face is no compensation for this defect. Moreover, the ugliest features, when accompanied by a symmetrical body, are absolutely preferred. Furthermore, we are most sensitive to every disproportion of the skeleton, as, for instance, a stunted, short-legged figure, *et al.*, also a limping gait, where it is not the result of an accident. On the other hand, a strikingly beautiful stature can compensate all defects: it bewitches us. Here may be mentioned the great stress which is laid upon a small foot: the reason is that this is an essential characteristic of the *genus*, for no animal has *tarsus* and *metatarsus*, taken together, so small as man; which is connected with his upright gait; he is a plantigrade. In accordance with this, Jesus Sirach (26-33) says: "A well-built woman with beautiful feet is like golden pillars on silver pedestals." The teeth, too, are important; because they are essential to nutrition, and especially inheritable. The fourth consideration is a certain *plumpness*, that is, a prominence of the vegetative function, plasticity, promising the foetus rich nourishment; therefore, undue leanness strongly repels us. A full female bosom has an uncommon charm for the male sex; because, standing in direct connection with her propagative functions, it promises the newly-born plenty of nourishment. Moreover, *excessively* fat women arouse our disgust; the cause of it is that such a constitution indicates atrophy of the uterus, that is, barrenness; which is known, not by the mind, but by instinct. The very last consideration is *beauty of features*. Here, too, the bony parts are the most important consideration. A beautiful nose is especially attractive, while a short, pug nose mars all.

The life's happiness of innumerable girls has been decided by a slight upward or downward curve of the nose; and rightly: for the type of the *genus* is at stake. A small mouth, as caused by small maxillaries, is very essential, being a specific characteristic of the human face in opposition to the mouths of beasts. A sunken, as it were, cut-away chin is particularly repugnant, because *mentum prominulum* is exclusively a trait of our species. Lastly, is the consideration of beautiful eyes and forehead: they are connected with the psychical, especially the intellectual, qualities which are inherited from the mother.

The unconscious considerations which govern the choice of women, we can, of course, not give so accurately. On the whole, the following may be maintained. Their choice is given to men of from thirty to thirty-five years of age; and, indeed, they prefer them to youths, although these represent the highest human beauty. The reason is, that they are guided, not by taste, but by instinct, which recognizes this age as the acme of generative power. In general, they care little for beauty, especially of the face: it appears that they take it upon themselves to bestow beauty upon the child. They are won principally by man's strength and the courage allied to it: for these promise generation of strong children and, at the same time, a brave defender of them. Every bodily defect of man, every deviation from the type, woman, as far as the child is concerned, can remove in generation by being perfect in those parts herself, or even excelling in the opposite direction. Those qualities alone are to be excepted which are peculiar to his sex, and which, therefore, the mother cannot give to the child; to these belong the masculine build of the skeleton, broad shoulders, narrow hips, straight legs, muscular power, courage, beard, etc. Thence it comes that women often love ugly men, but never an unmanly man; because they cannot neutralize his defects.

The second class of considerations which lie at the foundation of love, are the psychical qualities. Here we find that woman is attracted throughout by the qualities of his heart or character,—since they are inherited from the father. Preëminently, it is firmness of will, determination, and courage, perhaps, too, honesty and kindness of heart, which win women. Intellectual parts, however, exercise no direct and instinctive power over her, for the reason that they are not inherited from the father. Lack of brains is of no consequence to a woman; rather, excessive mental power, or even genius, being an abnormity, may operate unfavorably. Therefore, we often see an ugly, stupid, and rude man cut out a well-bred, talented, and amiable man. So, too, love-marriages are often concluded between intellectually very heterogenous beings; *e. g.*, *he*, rude, strong, and narrow-minded; *she*, tender, sensitive, discriminating, well-bred, æsthetic, etc.; or, *he*, even genial and learned; *she*, a goose:

> Sic visum Veneri; cui placet impares
> Formas atque animos sub juga aenea
> Saevo mittere cum joco.

The cause of it is that here not intellectual, but entirely different, considerations predominate—those of instinct. The object is not intellectual entertainment, but the generation of children: it is a union of hearts, not of heads. It is a vain and ridiculous pretence of women to assert that they have fallen in love with a man's mind, or it is the overstraining of a degenerate being. Men, on the other hand, are not influenced, in instinctive love, by the *qualities* of a woman's *character*. Therefore, so many a Socrates has found his Xantippe, as, for instance, Shakespeare, Albrecht Duerer, Byron. Here, however, *intellectual* qualities have influence, because they are inherited from the mother. Yet their influence is easily overbalanced by physical beauty, as this, touching more essential points, acts more immediately. And so it happens that mothers, feeling or having experienced that influence, have their daughters learn fine arts, languages, etc., to make them more attractive to men; whereby they wish to assist the intellect by artificial means as well as, in case of need, the hips and bosom. It must be borne in mind, that here we are speaking only of that wholly direct, instinctive attraction which alone is the source of real love. That an intelligent and educated woman prizes understanding and talent in a man; that a man, after reasonable reflection, examines and considers the character of his bride, has nothing whatever to do with the matter here in question: such things establish a reasonable choice in marriage, but not passionate love, which is our theme.

Hitherto, I have regarded only the *absolute* considerations, that is, such which apply to every one. I now come to the *relative* considerations which are individual, because they are intended to rectify the type of the *genus*, which is defectively represented in them, to correct the deviations from it, which the very person of the chosen carries with himself, and thus to lead back to the genuine representation of the type. In such cases, therefore, each one loves what he lacks. Starting from the individual constitution, and directed towards it, the choice resting upon such *relative* considerations is always much more definite, decided, and exclusive than the choice starting from merely absolute considerations. Therefore, the origin of real, passionate love, as a rule, will lie in these relative considerations, and only the origin of the common, lighter inclination, in the absolute considerations. In accordance with this, regular, perfect beauties are not wont to kindle great passion. In order that a truly passionate inclination may arise, something that can be expressed only by a chemical metaphor is necessary: two persons must neutralize each other as acid and alkali to form a base. The conditions necessary for this are, in the main, as follows: First, all sexuality is one-sidedness. This one-sidedness is more decidedly expressed and present in a higher degree in one individual than in another; therefore, in each one, it can be supplemented and neutralized better by one than by another individual of the opposite sex, because a one-sidedness individually opposed to his own is necessary to supplement the type of humanity in the new individual that is to be born, around whose make-up the whole matter turns. Physiologists know that masculineness and feminineness have innumerable degrees, within which the former sinks to the repulsive *gynander* and *hypospadæus*, the latter rises to the enchanting *androgyne:* from both sides complete hermaphrodism may be reached, upon which stand individuals who, being midway between both sexes, are to be counted with neither, consequently, are unfit to procreate. To the neutralization of the two individualities by one another, there is, accordingly, required that the definite degree of *his* masculineness exactly correspond to the definite degree of *her* feminineness, in order that both one-sidednesses may just balance one another. Accordingly, the manliest man will seek the womanliest woman, and *vice versa;* and so each will seek the one individually corresponding to him in the degree of sexuality. Now, how far the necessary relation exists between the two, is instinctively felt by them and lies, together with the other *relative* considerations, at the bottom of the higher degrees of love. While, therefore, the lovers are pathetically speaking of the harmony of their souls, most generally the harmony of the offspring, and his perfection, is the kernel of the matter, and, manifestly, is of much more importance than the harmony of their souls,—which often, not long after marriage, dissolves into a glaring disharmony. To this are joined the further relative considerations which rest upon each ones endeavor to balance his weaknesses, defects, and deviations from the type by the other, lest they are perpetuated in the offspring, or even augment to real abnormities. The weaker a man is in muscular strength, the more will he be attracted by strong women. The same holds true with woman. But since woman is by nature endowed with less muscular power, she will, as a rule, give the preference to the stronger man. Furthermore, size is an important consideration. Small men have a decided inclination for large women, and *vice versa;* and, indeed, in a small man, the predilection for large women will be the more passionate, in case he himself was begotten by a large father and remained small only through the influence of the mother; because he has inherited from the father the vascular system and its energy, which can supply a large body with blood; however, if his father and grandfather were small, that inclination will be less positively felt. The aversion that a large woman has for large men, is founded upon nature's intention to avoid too large a race, if it, with the powers to be imparted by this woman, would become too weak to live long. If, notwithstanding, such a woman chooses a large husband, perhaps in order to appear better in society, generally, their posterity will suffer for the folly. Another very decided consideration is complexion. Blondes positively demand brunettes; but seldom is the opposite true. The cause of it is that blonde hair and blue eyes are a kind of sport, almost an abnormity: analogous to white mice, or, at least, to white horses. They are native to no other part of the world, not even to the countries near the poles, with the exception of Europe. Evidently, they issued from Scandinavia. By the way, it is my opinion that white skin is not natural to man; but that he has by nature a black or brown skin as our forefathers, the Hindoos; that, consequently, a white man never sprang directly from the bosom of nature, and that there is no white race, much as may be spoken of it, but that every white man has become bleached. Driven into the north, where he is a foreigner, where he exists only like an exotic plant, and in winter needs, like them, the hothouse, man, in the course of thousands of years, grew white. The Gypsies, a Hindoo tribe, who emigrated about four centuries ago, show the transition from the complexion of the Hindoos to our own. In love, therefore, nature strives to return to dark hair and brown eyes as the original type; white skin, however, has become a second nature, though not so much so that the brown color of the Hindoos is repulsive to us. Lastly, each one seeks in the several parts of the body the corrective of his own defects and deviations, and the more decided, the more important the part is. Therefore, snub-nosed individuals take an inexpressible delight in hawk-noses: it is so with regard to all other parts. Men of excessively lank, long body and constitution, can find beautiful even an unduly compressed and shortened figure. Considerations of temperament operate analogously: each will prefer a temperament opposed to his own; though only in so far as his own is a decided one. He who is very perfect in any one respect, seeks and loves, indeed, not imperfection in this particular respect, but is reconciled to it more easily than another; because he himself preserves the children from great imperfection in these parts. For instance, who is very white himself will take no offense at a yellowish color of the face: but one of the latter color will find dazzling whiteness divinely beautiful. The rare case of a man's falling in love with a positively ugly woman, occurs, when the exact harmony of the degree of their sexuality existing, all her abnormities are just the opposite, consequently, the corrective of his own. In such cases, love is wont to reach a high degree.

The deep earnestness with which we scrutinize every part of a woman's body,— she on her part doing the same,— the critical scrupulousness with which we scan a woman who begins to please us, the willfulness of our choice, the strained attention with which a bridegroom observes his bride, his caution to be deceived in no part, and the great stress which he lays upon all details in the essential parts — all this fully corresponds to the importance of the object. For the child, during his whole life, will bear a similar part; for example, if the woman is but a little one-sided, this can easily burden her son with a hunch-back; and so in all other cases. Of course, there is no consciousness of all this; on the contrary, each one imagines he is making that difficult choice only in the interest of his own pleasure (which, in reality, cannot at all have a share in it). Nevertheless, taking for granted his own organization, he makes a selection entirely in the interest of the *genus*, to preserve whose type as purely as possible is the secret task. The individual here acts, without knowing it, as an agent for a higher, the *genus:* hence the importance that he attributes to things which as such would, nay, must be, wholly indifferent to him. There is something very peculiar in the deep, unconscious earnestness with which two young people of different sex, who see themselves for the first time, look at each other; in the searching and penetrating glance they cast at one another; in the critical examination, which all traits and parts of their persons must mutually undergo. Indeed, this scrutiny is *meditation of the genius of the genus* upon the individual possible through them, and the combination of his qualities. The intensity of their delight in, and longing for, one another, is determined by the result of that scrutiny. This desire, after having reached quite a height, may suddenly be quenched by the discovery of something which previously remained unnoticed. So, in all who are capable of generation, the genius of the *genus* meditates the coming race, whose composition is the great work with which *Cupid*, incessantly active, speculating, and pondering, is occupied. Compared with the importance of his great affair which concerns the *genus* and all coming generations, the affairs of individuals, in their whole ephemeral totality, are very trivial: therefore, he is always ready to sacrifice them regardlessly. For he stands to them in the relation of an immortal to a mortal, and his interests to theirs as infinite to finite. Thus, conscious of managing affairs of a higher order than those which concern merely individual weal and woe, he is engaged in them with sublime indifference: in the rush of war, in the whirl of business, or in the raging of a plague, and prosecutes them in the solitude of the cloister.

We saw in the above that the intensity of love grows with individualization, when we proved how it is possible for the physical constitution of two individuals to be such that, in order to restore as well as possible the type of the *genus*, one is the special and perfect supplement of the other. In this case, quite a passion arises, which, by the very fact that it is directed upon a single object, and only upon this, consequently, as though appearing in the *special* service of the *genus*, at once gains a nobler and sublimer tinge. On the other hand, mere sexual instinct is base; because, being without individualization, it is directed upon all, and strives to preserve the *genus* merely as regards quantity, without regard to quality. Now, however, individualization, and with it, intensity of love, can reach so high a degree that, without its gratification, all the good things of the world, nay, life itself, lose their worth. Then it is a wish becoming so violent that it surpasses all others; hence it prepares him for every sacrifice, and, in case fulfillment is inexorably denied, may lead him to insanity or suicide. Beside the unconscious considerations lying at the bottom of all passionate love, which have been heretofore mentioned, there must be others which we cannot perceive so clearly. We must, therefore, assume that here not only the organization, but also the *will* of the man and the *intellect* of the woman have a special appropriateness for one another, in consequence of which they alone can beget a particular individual, whose existence the genius of the *genus* here intends, for reasons which, as they lie in the essence of the thing *per se*, are inaccessible to us. Or, more strictly speaking: the will to live here wishes to objectivate itself in a certain definite individual who can be begotten by this father and this mother only. This metaphysical craving of the will *per se* has, at first, no other sphere of action in the chain of beings than the hearts of the future parents, who, accordingly, are seized with this desire, and now fancy they are wishing for their own sake what has merely a purpose for the present purely metaphysical; that is, lying outside of the chain of really existing things. Thus, the blind desire springing from the fountainhead of all beings, the desire of the unborn child to enter life, it is, which appears as the strong passion of the future parents for one another; which considers everything save itself a trifle; in fact, an illusion without equal, by virtue of which a man in love would give all the wealth in the world to sleep with this woman, who, in truth, accomplishes no more for him than any other woman. That, nevertheless, nothing else is intended, is evident from the fact that this strong passion, too, as well as every other, dies away in its enjoyment, to the great astonishment of the participants. This passion is also quenched, when, on account of the woman's barrenness (arising, according to Hufeland, from nineteen accidental constitutional defects), the real metaphysical purpose is frustrated; as daily occurs to millions of crushed germs, in whom the same metaphysical life-principle struggles to exist, wherein there is no other consolation, than that to the will to live there stands open an eternity of space, time, matter, and, consequently, an inexhaustible opportunity to return to life.

An insight into this must have, though fugitively, floated before the mind of Theophrastus Paracelsus, who has not treated this theme, and to whom my entire train of thought is foreign, when he, in quite a different context and in his desultory manner, wrote the following remarkable utterance: "*Hi sunt, quos Deus copulavit, ut eam, quae fuit Uriae et David; quamvis ex diametro (sic enim sibi humana mens persuadebat) cum justo et legitimo matrimonio pugnaret hoc.—sed propter Salomonem, qui aliunde nasci non potuit, nisi ex Bathseba, conjuncto David semine, quamvis meretrice, conjunxit eos Deus. (De vita longa,* 1, 5.) "There are some united by God, as, for instance, the wife of Urias and David, although conflicting directly with a just and legitimate marriage (for this is the conviction of humanity). But for Solomon's sake, who could not have been born otherwise than from Bathsheba and David, though she was an adulteress, God joined them."

Love's longing, ἵμερος, in expressing which in countless forms the poets of all times are incessantly engaged, and do not exhaust the subject; nay, cannot do justice to it;—this longing which connects the possession of a certain woman with the idea of an infinite bliss and an unutterable grief with the idea that she cannot be his,—this longing and grief of love cannot take their origin from the necessities of an ephemereal individual; but they are the sighs of the genius of the *genus* that here sees irreparable means of gaining or losing his purposes, and therefore deeply groans. The *genus* alone has infinite life, and hence is capable of infinite wishes, infinite gratifications, and infinite pain. But these are locked up in the narrow breast of a mortal; no wonder, then, that it would seem to burst, and can find no expression for the foreboding of infinite joy or of infinite woe. This, then, furnishes the material to all erotic poetry of a sublime cast, which, accordingly, scales heaven in metaphors transcending everything earthly. This is the theme of Petrarch, the material to the St. Preuxs, Werther and Jacopo Ortis, who otherwise could not be understood nor explained. For that esteem cannot rest upon intellectual, or at all upon objective, real merits of the beloved one; because, indeed, the lover is frequently but superficially acquainted with her, as was the case with Petrarch. The spirit of the *genus* alone is able to see at a glance of what *value* she is to the *genus* for its purposes. Likewise, great passions usually arise at first sight.

"Who ever loved who loved not at first sight?"
—*Shakespeare, A. Y. L. I., III.*, 5.

In this respect, there is a remarkable passage in the romance *Guzman de Alfarache,* by Mateo Aleman, which has been famous for two hundred and fifty years: "*No es necessario, para que uno ame, que pase distancia de tiempo, que siga discurso, ni haga eleccion, sino, que con aquella primera y sola vista, concurran junctamente cierta correspondencia o consonancia o lo que aca solemos vulgarmente decir, una confrontacion de sangre, a que por particular influxo suelen mover las estrellas.*" "In order to love it is not necessary for much time to pass, or for him to reflect and make a choice, but only, that, at that first and single glance, a certain mutual fitness and harmony meet, or, what we, in common life, are wont to call a *sympathy* of blood, and which is wont to be favored by a peculiar influence of the heavenly bodies." And so, loss of the beloved one by a rival, or by death, is to the passionate lover a grief surpassing every other, just because it is of a transcendent nature; for it concerns him not as an individual only, but also attacks him in his *essentia eterna*, the life of the *genus*, in whose special will and commission he was here engaged. Therefore, jealousy is so tormenting and fierce, and relinquishing the beloved one, the greatest of all sacrifices. A hero is ashamed of all lamentation except in love; because in this not he, but the *genus*, wails. In Calderon's *Great Zenobia*, there is, in the second act, a scene between Zenobia and Decius, who says:

> "Cielos, luego to me quieres?
> Perdiera cien mil victorias,
> Volvierame," etc.

"O Heaven! do you love me! For this I would surrender a hundred thousand victories, would return," etc. Here honor, which hitherto outweighed every interest, is driven from the field as soon as love, that is, the interest of the *genus*, comes into play and sees a decided advantage: for this is infinitely superior to every interest of mere individuals, no matter how important. Therefore, to it alone honor, duty, and faith, give way, after they have resisted every other. temptation, even the menace of death. So, too, we find, in private life, that conscience is nowhere found so seldom as in this matter: it is set aside sometimes by otherwise honest and just people, and adultery regardlessly committed, when passionate love, that is, the interest of the *genus*, has taken possession of them. It seems, indeed, as though they believed themselves conscious of a higher authority than the interest of individuals can ever lend, for the very reason that they act in the interest of the *genus*. Remarkable in this respect are the words of Chamfort: "*Quand un homme et une femme out l' un pour l' autre une passion violente, il me semble toujours que, quelque soient les obstacles que les séparent, un mari, des parens, etc., les deux amans sont l' un a l' autre, de par la Nature, qu' ils s' appartiennent de droit divin, malgré les lois et les conventions humanies.*" "When a man and a woman have a violent passion for one another, it always seems to me, whatever the obstacles separating them may be, as husband, parents, that the two lovers are for one another by nature, that they belong to each other by divine right, in spite of human laws and conventions." Who would take offense at this, will have to be referred to the striking leniency which the Saviour in the Gospel observes toward the adulteress, as he takes for granted the same guilt in all present. From this standpoint, the greater part of the *Decameron* appears as a mere mockery and scoff of the genius of the *genus* at the down-trodden rights and interests of individuals. With equal ease, all differences of cast and all similar relations, when they are opposed to the union of passionate lovers, are set aside and declared null and void by the genius of the *genus*, who, pursuing his purpose pertaining to endless generations, scatters like chaff such opinions and scruples of man. For the same deep-rooted reason, when the purposes of this passion are at stake, every danger is willingly brooked, and even the otherwise pusillanimous then becomes courageous. Likewise, in dramas and romances, we observe, with joy and sympathy, young people fighting for their love-affairs, that is, the interest of the *genus*, and gaining the victory over the old folks, who consider merely the welfare of individuals. For the efforts of lovers appear to us much more momentous, sublime, and just, than any opposing them; as the *genus* is more important than the individual. Accordingly, the principal theme of nearly all comedies is the appearance of the genius of the *genus* and his purposes, which run counter to the personal interests of the characters represented, and therefore threaten to undermine their happiness. As a rule, it is a success, which, being in accordance with poetic justice, satisfies the spectator, because he feels that the purposes of the *genus* surpass those of the individuals. Therefore, at the end, he confidently deserts the victorious lovers, sharing with them the illusion that they have established their own happiness, which, rather, they have sacrificed to the welfare of the *genus*, in opposition to the will of the cautious elders. In a few abnormal comedies, it has been tried to reverse the matter and to achieve the happiness of the individuals at the expense of the purposes of the *genus*: but here the spectator feels the pain which the genius of the *genus* suffers, and is not consoled by the advantages which the individuals secure. As examples of this class, I have in mind a few very well-known plays: *La reine de 16 ans*, and *Le mariage de raison*. In love-tragedies, where the purposes of the *genus* are frustrated, the lovers, who were its tools, usually perish together: as in Romeo and Juliet, Tancred, Don Carlos, Wallenstein, Bride of Messina.

Human love furnishes often comic, oftentimes tragic, phenomena; both, because possessed of the spirit of the *genus*, man is now swayed by him and is no longer himself: thereby his actions become inappropriate to the individual. In the highest degrees of love, what gives his thoughts so poetic and sublime a tinge, even a transcendent and hyperphysical turn, by virtue of which he seems altogether to lose sight of his true purpose, is, at bottom, due to the fact that he is now animated by the spirit of the *genus*, whose affairs are infinitely more important than all those concerning mere individuals, in order to lay, in its special commission, the foundation to the existence of an indefinitely long posterity, of *this* individual and definite constitution. Posterity can receive this only from him as father and his beloved one as mother. Otherwise it, *as such*, never enters life, while the objectivation of the will to live expressly demands its existence. It is the feeling that one is acting in affairs of such transcendent importance which exalts the lover above all earthly things, yea, above himself, and gives his very physical wishes such a hyperphysical dress, that love becomes a poetic episode even in the life of the most prosaic. In the latter case, the affair at times has a comical aspect. This commission of the will, objectivating itself in the *genus*, is represented in the consciousness of the lover under the mask of anticipation of an infinite bliss, to be found in the union with this woman. In the highest degrees of love, this chimera becomes so gorgeous, that, in case she cannot be won, life itself loses all charms, and then appears so joyless, shallow, and unpalatable, that the disgust of it conquors even the terrors of death: hence it is sometimes voluntarily shortened. The will of such a man has been drawn into the whirlpool of the will of the *genus*, or, this has so gained the supremacy over the individual will, that, if the latter cannot be active for the *genus*, it disdains to be active for the individual. The individual is here too weak a vessel to bear the infinite longing of the will of the *genus*, concentrated upon a certain object. In this case the issue is suicide; sometimes the double suicide of both lovers; unless nature, in order to save life, causes insanity, which then enshrouds with its veil the consciousness of that hopeless condition. No year passes by without proving, by several cases, the truth of this.

Not only has unsatisfied passion frequently a tragic end, but also, when gratified, leads more often to unhappiness than to happiness. For its demands often conflict so strongly with the personal welfare of the interested, that they undermine it by being irreconcilable to his other relations, and destroying the plan of life built upon them. Indeed, love runs counter, not only to all external relations, but even to the individuality itself, by throwing itself upon persons, who, outside of sexual relation, are hateful, despicable, nay, disgusting, to the lover. But so much more powerful is the will of the *genus* than the individual's, that the lover closes his eyes to all those repugnant qualities, overlooks all, misknows all, and forever unites himself with the object of his passion. So completely is he blinded by that illusion, which, as soon as the will of the *genus* is fulfilled, vanishes and leaves behind a hated companion for life. Only from this can it be explained that we so often see reasonable, even distinguished, men united to dragons and matrimonial devils, and we cannot understand how they could have made such a choice. On this account, the ancients represented Amor as blind. Indeed, the lover can even recognize and bitterly feel the intolerable defects of the temperament and character of his bride, promising him a life of torment, and yet not be frightened:

> "I ask not, I care not,
>   If guilt's in thy heart;
> I know that I love thee
>   Whatever thou art."

For, in reality, he is working not for his own, but for the cause of a third who is yet to be born; although he is possessed of the illusion that he is working for his own cause. But this very not-working-for one's own cause, which is everywhere the stamp of greatness, gives a tinge of the sublime also to passionate love, and makes it a worthy subject of poetry. Finally, love and extreme hatred of the beloved one may exist together; therefore, Plato compared it to the love of wolves for sheep. This is the case, when a passionate lover, in spite of all efforts and entreaties, can, under no condition, obtain a hearing:

> "I love and hate her."
> —*Shakespeare, Cym., II.,* 5.

The hatred of the beloved one which is then kindled, may excite him to murder her and then himself. A few examples of this class are wont to happen every year: they are to be found in the newspapers. Therefore Goethe's verse is very true:

> "Bei aller verschmæhten Liebe! beim hœllischen Elemente!
> Ich wollt', ich wuesst' was ærger's dass ich's fluchen kœnnte!"

> "By all love ever rejected! By hell-fire hot and unsparing!
> I wish I knew something worse, that I might use it for swearing!"

It is indeed no hyperbole, when a lover denotes as *cruelty* the coldness of the beloved one and the pleasure of her vanity which takes delight in his sufferings. For he is under the impulse of an instinct, which, being related to the instinct of insects, forces him, in spite of all reasons, to prosecute its purpose at all hazards, and regard everything else as secondary: he cannot desist. Not one, but many a Petrarch has lived, who was compelled to drag all his life unsatisfied longing of love, as fetters, as a block of iron on his foot, and to heave his sighs in solitary forests, but only in that one Petrarch there dwelt poetic power; so that Goethe's beautiful verse is true of him:

> "Und wenn der Mensch in seiner Quaal verstummt,
> Gab mir ein Gott, zu sagen, wie ich leide."

In fact, the genius of the *genus* everywhere wages war with the guardian geniuses of the individuals, is their persecutor and enemy, always ready to mercilessly sacrifice personal happiness in order to accomplish his purposes: indeed, the welfare of whole nations has at times become the victim of his humor: an example of this kind Shakespeare has given us in Henry VI., Part III., Act. 3, Sc. 2-3. All this rests upon the fact that the *genus*, in which our being is rooted, has a nearer and earlier claim upon us than the individual; hence, its affairs take precedence. Feeling this, the ancients personified the genius of the *genus* in Cupid, a god who, in spite of his childish appearance, was a capricious, despotic demon, but nevertheless lord of gods and men:

συ, δ'ω 9εων τυραννε κ'ανϑρωπων, Ερως!

"Thou, tyrant of gods and men, Eros!"

Murderous missile, blindness, and wings are his attributes. The latter indicate fickleness; which, as a rule, begins with disappointment, the result of gratification.

Because this passion is founded upon an illusion representing that which is of value only to the *genus*, as valuable to the individual, the illusion must vanish after the purpose of the *genus* has been gained. The spirit of the *genus*, who took possession of the individual, liberates him again. Deserted by the spirit, he relapses into his original narrowness and poverty, and beholds with astonishment that, after such great, heroic, and infinite efforts, nothing more fell to his share of enjoyment than what every other sexual gratification yields: contrary to his expectations, he finds himself no happier than before. He perceives that he has been the dupe of the will of the *genus*. Therefore, as a rule, a Theseus, when gratified, will desert his Ariadne. Had Petrarch's passion been satisfied, his song thenceforth would have become mute, as the bird's, as soon as it has laid its eggs.

I may remark, by the way, that strongly as my metaphysics of love must displease those who are at the time swayed by this passion, nevertheless, if, against love reason can avail ought, the fundamental truth disclosed by me, must, sooner than anything else, enable them to overpower it. But, no doubt, the words of the old comic poet will hold true: *"Quae res in se neque consilium, neque modum habet ullum, eam consilio regere non potes."* "That which in itself possesses neither reason or order, you cannot govern by reason."

Love-marriages are concluded in the interest of the *genus*, not of individuals. The participants, it is true, imagine they are promoting their own happiness: but the real object they are entirely ignorant of, it being an individual whom they alone can beget. Brought together by this purpose, they ought henceforth to endeavor to get along with each other as well as possible. But very often the couple united by that instinctive illusion, which is the essence of passionate love, will be of the most heterogeneous character. This appears as soon as the illusion vanishes, as it needs must. Accordingly, love-marriages usually turn out unhappily: for, by them, the coming is cared for at the expense of the present generation. "*Quien se casa por amores, ha de vivir con dolores.*" "Who marries for love must live in grief," says the Spanish proverb. The opposite holds true of marriages concluded for the sake of convenience, generally according to the choice of the parents. The considerations here influencing them, of whatever sort they may be, are at least real, and cannot disappear of their own accord. In this case, the happiness of the present generation is provided for, but, indeed, to the detriment of posterity; still the former remains problematic. The man who, in marriage, looks more to money than to satisfy his inclination, lives more in the individual than in the *genus;* which is diametrically opposed to the truth; hence it appears contrary to nature, and rouses a certain contempt of him. A girl who, in opposition to the advice of her parents, refuses a man who is rich and not old, and ignores all consideration of convenience, in order to choose according to her instinctive inclination only, sacrifices her individual welfare for the welfare of the *genus*. But, for this very reason, a certain approbation cannot be denied her: for she has preferred the more important, and acted in the sense of nature, more nearly, of the *genus*, while the parents advised her in the sense of individual egoism. Accordingly, it seems that, in marriages, either the individual, or the interest of the *genus*, must suffer. Usually, such is the case: for, that convenience and passionate love go hand in hand, is the rarest streak of luck. The wretched condition of most persons, physically, morally, and intellectually, may partially be caused by the fact that marriages are usually concluded, not from pure choice and inclination, but from all sorts of external considerations, and according to accidental circumstances. But if, in addition to convenience, inclination is, to a certain extent, taken into consideration, this is, as it were, a settlement with the genius of the *genus*. Happy marriages, we all know, are rare; because it lies in the nature of marriage that its principal object is not the present but the coming generation. However, I may add for the consolation of tender and loving souls, that a feeling of very different origin is sometimes associated with passionate love; namely, real friendship, founded upon harmony of sentiments. Still, this friendship usually does not appear until sexual love has died out. This friendship will generally arise from the fact that the physical, moral, and intellectual qualities, which correspond to and supplement each other with regard to the child, will supplement one another also with reference to the individuals themselves, as opposite qualities of temperament and intellectual advantages; thereby a harmony of sentiments is founded.

The entire metaphysics of love here treated stands in close connection with my metaphysics in general, and the light which it reflects upon this may be summed up in the following:

We have learned, that, in the gratification of sexual instinct, the careful selection rising through innumerable gradations to passionate love, rests upon the very sincere interest which man takes in the special personal constitution of the coming generation. This most remarkable interest confirms two truths laid down in the preceding chapter: first, the indestructibility of man's being *per se*, which continues to live in the coming race. For, that lively and eager interest, springing not from reflection and intention, but from the innermost trait and instinct of our being, could not exist so indestructibly and exercise so great power over man, if he were absolutely transitory, and a generation really and entirely different from him, succeeded him merely in point of time. Secondly, that his being *per se* lies more in the *genus* than in the individual. For, that interest in the special constitution of the *genus*, which is the root of all love-matters, from the most fleeting inclination to the most earnest passion is, after all, the most important affair to each one; that is, the success or failure of which touches him most sensitively; hence it is preëminently called the *affair of the heart*. Likewise, for this interest, when it is expressed strongly and decidedly, every personal interest is neglected, and, when necessary, sacrificed. Thereby, then, man bears witness to the greater interest he takes in the *genus*, than in the individual, and to the fact that he lives more immediately in the former than in the latter. Why, then, does the lover hang with perfect devotion on the eyes of his beloved one, and is ready to sacrifice anything for her sake. Because it is his *immortal* part that craves for her: only his mortal part it is that craves for everything else.

That lively, or even fervent, longing concentrated upon a particular woman is, accordingly, an immediate pledge of the indestructibility of the kernel of our being and its persistence in the *genus*. However, to take this persistence for something trivial and unsatisfactory, is an error arising from the fact that, under the persistence of the *genus*, we think nothing more than the future existence of beings similar to, but in no wise identical with, us; and this again, because, starting from the cognition directed to the external world, one considers only the outer forms of the *genus* as we intuitively apprehend it, and not its inner essence. But this very inner essence it is, which, as its kernel, lies at the bottom of our own consciousness; therefore, it is even more immediate than our consciousness itself, and, being the thing *per se*, free from the principle of individuation, is really the same and identical in all individuals, whether they are side by side or follow one another. Now this is the will to live, the very thing which so urgently craves for life and persistence. Accordingly, it is safe from, and untouched by, death. But, furthermore, it can attain to no condition better than the present: whence it follows, that, while there is life, it is sure of the sufferings and death of individuals. To free it from this, is reserved for the *denial* of the will to live, by which the individual will tears itself away from the *genus*, and ceases to live in it.

We lack all ideas, nay, all data, as to what it then is. We can but designate it as that which has the liberty to be or not to be will to live. In the latter instance, Buddhism designates it by the name of *Nirvana*, whose etymology has been given at the close of chapter forty-one. It is that point which forever remains inaccessible to all human cognition as such.

When now, from the standpoint of this last consideration, we gaze upon the tumult of life, we behold all busied with its distress and evils, exerting all powers to satisfy the endless wants, and to ward off the manifold suffering, and still without daring to hope anything else than the very preservation of this tormented individual existence for a brief space of time. In the midst of all this turmoil, however, we behold the yearning glances of two lovers meeting; but why so secretly, timidly, and stealthily? Because these lovers are the traitors secretly endeavoring to perpetuate all this distress and drudgery, that otherwise would reach a timely end; which they would wish to frustrate as their ancestors have formerly done.

GENIUS.

THAT manner of cognition,* from which all genuine works of art, of poetry, and even of philosophy, originate, is, when preponderating, designated by the name of genius. As the subject matter of this manner of cognition is the Platonic *ideas*, these, however, being conceived of not abstractly, but *intuitively only*, the essence of genius must consist in the perfection and energy of *intuitive* cognition. Corresponding to this, we hear such most emphatically pronounced works of genius as proceed immediately from intuition, and appeal to intuition, that is, the works of the plastic arts, and next, those of poetry, which imparts its intuitions through the imagination. Even here the difference between genius and mere talent is perceptible. The latter is an advantage lying more in the greater adroitness and acutenes of the discursive than of the intuitive cognition. Who is endowed with it, thinks more rapidly and correctly than the rest. Genius, however, beholds an alto-

---

* Described in "Welt als Wille und Vorstellung." Vol. II., Chap. 29, 30.

gether different world, though only by gazing deeper into the one lying before them as well, because the world is represented in his mind more objective, consequently, purer and clearer.

The intellect, according to its destiny, is merely the medium of motives: accordingly, it originally sees no more in things than their relations to the will,—the direct, the indirect, the possible. In animals, where the motives are almost all direct, the matter is therefore most obvious: what does not concern their will, does not exist for them. Hence we sometimes see with astonishment that even sagacious animals do not notice something striking in itself, for instance, visible changes in our person or surroundings. In the normal man, the indirect and possible relations to the will are added, whose sum constitutes useful knowledge; but here, too, cognition is still concerned with *relations.* For this very reason, no quite purely objective picture of things is formed in the normal man; because his intuitive power, as soon as it is not spurred on and set in motion by the will, immediately relapses and becomes inactive, for it has not energy enough to conceive of the world, by its own elasticity, purely objectively and *without a purpose.* However, where this happens, where the representing power of the brain has such a surplus that a pure, distinct, objective picture of the outside world is formed *without a purpose,*—a picture, which is useless for the purposes of the will, and in the higher degrees, a hinderance, nay, which can even be an injury to them;—there at least the predisposition to that abnormity exists, which is denoted by the name of *genius*, indicating that here something foreign to the will, that is, to the real ego, as though it were a *genius* coming from the outside, seems to become active. But, to speak without a metaphor, genius consists in a development of the intuitive faculty considerably greater than is necessary for the *service of the will*, for which alone it was originally intended. Therefore, with strictness, physiology, could, in a certain measure, class such a surplus of brain-activity, and of brain itself, with the *monstris per excessum*, which, as is well known, it classes with the *monstris per defectum*, and those *per situm mutatum*. Genius, then, consists in an abnormal excess of intellect, which can find employment only by being directed upon existence in general; so that it is in the service of the whole human race, as the normal intellect in the service of the individual. To make the matter clearer, we could say: if the normal man is composed of two-thirds will and one-third intellect, then genius is two-thirds intellect and one-third will. This might further be illustrated by a chemical simile: 'the base and the acid of a neutral salt differ from one another in this, that, in each of the two, radical and oxygen stand in converse relation. It is a base or alkali, when the radical preponderates over the oxygen, and it is an acid when the oxygen preponderates. In like manner, as regards will and intellect, the normal man and the genius are related. From this, then, arises between them a fundamental difference which is visible in all their being and actions, but especially becomes manifest in their achievements. While, however, that total opposition between chemical substances causes the strongest affinity and attraction for one another, rather the contrary is wont to happen among the human race.

The first expression called forth by such a surplus of the power of cognition is shown generally in the most original and fundamental form of cognition, *i. e.*, the *intuitive*, and causes the repetition of the latter in a picture: this is the origin of the painter and sculptor. In these, the path from the conception of the genius to the production of the artist is shortest: therefore, the form in which genius and its activity are here manifested, is simplest, and its description easiest. However, we have here explained the source, whence all genuine productions in every art, even in poetry and philosophy, take their origin, though the process is not so simple.

Remember the result obtained in the first book, that all intuition is intellectual, and not merely sensual. Adding to this the former explanation and, at the same time, fairly considering that the philosophy of the last century designated the intuitive power of cognition by the name of "lower powers of the soul," we will not find it so wholly absurd, nor worthy of the bitter scorn with which Jean Paul, in his Preparatory School of Æsthetics, quotes it, that Adelung, who had to speak the language of his age, placed genius in "a considerable strength of the lower powers of the soul." Great as are the merits of the above mentioned work of this admirable man, I must still remark, that wherever theoretical explanation and instruction in general are the object, a discourse continually affecting wit and crowded with similes, is hardly appropriate.

It is *intuition*, to which primarily the real and true essence of things, though conditionally, is revealed. All ideas, all thought, are, indeed, mere abstractions, consequently partial representations from it, and have arisen merely by abstracting. All profound cognition, even real wisdom, roots in the *intuitive* apprehension of things; which has been considered in detail in the supplement to the first book. An *intuitive* apprehension has always been the generative process, in which every genuine work of art, every immortal thought received the spark of life: all original thinking is done in pictures. From *ideas*, however, arise the works of mere talent, merely reasonable thoughts, imitations, and generally all that is destined only for present emergency and contemporaries. However, if our intuition were always limited to the real presence of objects, its material would stand wholly under the sway of chance, which seldom presents things at the right moment, seldom arranges them suitably, and usually offers them to us in very defective specimens. Therefore, *imagination* is needed, in order to complete, arrange, embellish, fix, and reproduce at pleasure all the significant pictures of life, as the purposes of a deeply penetrating cognition and of the significant work, by which it is to be imparted, may require. Upon this rests the great value of the imagination, an indispensable tool to genius. For by means of it alone he is enabled, according to the requirements of the association of his sculpturing, composing, or thinking, to bring before his mind every object or event in a lively picture, and so always draw fresh nourishment from the original fountain-head of all cognition, the real world. Who is gifted with imagination may, as it were, call forth ghosts, revealing to him, at the proper time, the truths which the naked reality of objects furnishes but feebly, rarely, and then usually importunely. He is related to the unimaginative as the fleet, nay, winged animal to the cockle, moored to its rock, that must wait for what chance may bring it. For the unimaginative knows none but the real, sensuous intuition: until it comes, he gnaws upon ideas and abstractions, that are at best but the shells and husks, not the kernel, of cognition. He will never accomplish anything great, except perhaps in ciphering and mathematics. The works of the plastic arts, and of poetry, as well as the performance of mimicry, can also be looked upon as means of replacing as much as possible the lack of imagination to the unimaginative, and of facilitating its use to those gifted with it.

Although the peculiar and essential manner of the cognition of genius is the *intuitive*, nevertheless, its subject-matter is by no means the single objects, but the Platonic ideas expressed in them, the apprehension of which has been analyzed in the twenty-ninth chapter. It is a fundamental trait of genius always to see the general in the particular; while the normal man recognizes in single things only the single thing as such; for only as such it belongs to that reality which alone interest his *will*, that is, stands in relation to it. The degree in which every one not merely thinks, but directly beholds, in a particular object, only this object, or something more or less general, up to the most general of the genus, is the measure of his approximation to genius. Corresponding to this, only the essence of things in general, the general in them, the whole, is the real subject-matter of genius: the investigation of the single phenomena is the field of talent, as in the real sciences, whose subject-matter is throughout merely the relations of things to one another.

What was shown at length in a preceding chapter, namely, that the apprehension of the ideas is thereby conditioned, that the thinking faculty be the *pure subject* of cognition, that is, the will must wholly disappear from the consciousness, must here be borne in mind. The pleasure we take in some of Goethe's songs, bringing the landscape before our eyes, or in Jean Paul's descriptions of nature, rests upon the fact that we then share the objectivity of those minds, that is, the purity with which in them the world as representation was severed and, as it were, wholly separated from the world as will. From the fact that the manner of cognition of the genius is essentially one purified from all will and its relations, it follows that his works arise not intentionally or willfully, but that he is led by a sort of instinctive necessity. What is called the stirrings of genius, the hour of consecration, the moment of inspiration, is nothing but the liberation of the intellect, when the latter, for the time exempt from service to the will, does not now sink into inactivity or relaxation, but, for a short time, is active all alone, of its own accord. Then the intellect is of the greatest purity, and becomes the true mirror of the world: for, wholly separated from its origin, the will, it is now the world as representation itself, concentrated in *one* consciousness. In such moments, as it were, the soul of immortal works is begotten. On the other hand, in all intentional meditation, the intellect is not free; for the will leads it and prescribes its theme.

The stamp of commonness, the expression of vulgarity, which is impressed upon most faces, consists really in this, that the strict subordination of their cognition to their will, the firm chain linking both together, and the impossibility arising in consequence to view things otherwise than in relation to the will and its purposes, is visible upon them. On the contrary, the expression of genius, which forms the family resemblance of all highly gifted minds, lies in this, that the acquittal, the manumission of the intellect from the service of the will, the predominance of cognition over will may be clearly read upon them: and because all pain arises from will, cognition as such, however, being painless and serene; this gives to their lofty foreheads and contemplative gaze, which are not subject to the service of the will and its distress, that tinge of great, as it were, unearthly, hilarity, which at times breaks through and agrees very well with the melancholy of the other features, especially of the mouth. In this respect, it may be strikingly designated by the motto of Gordanus Bruno: "*In tristitia hilaris, in hilaritate, tristis.*" "Joyous in sadness, sad in joy."

The will, which is the root of the intellect, opposes all activity of the intellect, except that which serves its purposes. Therefore, the intellect is capable of a purely objective and profound apprehension of the external world, only when it is severed at least temporarily from its root. While the intellect is still united to it, it is of its own accord not at all capable of activity, but sleeps in lethargy, as often as the will (interest) does not awaken it and set it in motion. Where this is the case, it is indeed very fit to recognize, in accordance with the interest of the will, the relations of things, as the prudent mind does, who must always be wide awake, that is, stimulated by the will; but, for this very reason, he is not able to apprehend the purely objective essence of things. For, his will and purposes make him so one-sided that he sees in things only what concerns them; the remainder, however, partly vanishing, partly entering the consciousness in a vitiated condition. For instance, a man traveling in fear and haste will behold the Rhine and its shores but as a cross-road, and the bridge over it as another. In the mind of the man who is occupied with his aims, the world appears like a beautiful landscape upon the plan of a battle-field. Of course, these are extremes taken for the sake of clearness: but every excitement of the will, however slight, will cause a slight, though always analagous, corruption of cognition. In its true color and form, in its entire and true significance, the world can stand forth not until the intellect, rid of the will, floats free above objects and, without being influenced by the will, is still intensely active. Of course, this is opposed to the nature and destiny of the intellect, that is, it is, to a certain extent, contrary to nature, hence so very rare: but in this very thing lies the essence of genius, in which alone that condition occurs in a high degree and continuously, while in others only approximately and exceptionally. In this sense I take it when Jean

Paul (Preparatory School of Æsthetics, Par. 12) put the essence of genius in *profound contemplation* (Besonnenheit). For, the normal man is buried in the whirl and tumult of life, to which he is bound by his will: his intellect is wholly filled with the things and events of life: but of these things and of life in their objective significance he does not at all become aware; as a merchant on 'Change at Amsterdam perceives very well what his neighbor says, but does not hear the hum of the whole exchange, resembling the roar of the sea and astounding the distant observer. Private affairs do not hide the world and the things themselves from the genius, whose intellect is severed from the will, that is, the person; but he becomes clearly aware of them, he perceives them as such in objective intuition: in this sense he is *profoundly contemplative*.

It is this *profound contemplation* which enables the painter to reproduce faithfully on his canvas the nature which lies before him, and the poet to recall, by means of abstract ideas, exactly the reality once observed, and so give expression to it and bring it distinctly before our consciousness; likewise, to express in words what others merely feel. Animals live without any contemplation; they have consciousness, that is, they are cognizant of their weal and woe, as well as of the objects causing it. But their cognition never becomes objective; it always remains subjective. All within its range seems to them a matter of course, and can, therefore, never become an object of representation or a problem (object of meditation) to them. Hence, their consciousness is wholly *immanent*. Though not of equal, yet of related, nature, is the consciousness of the great mass of mankind, inasmuch as their perception of things and of the world remains predominantly subjective and immanent. They perceive the things in the world, but not the world; their own action and suffering, but not themselves. Now, as the clearness of consciousness increases in infinite gradations, profound contemplation appears more and more, and so, gradually, a point is reached where at times (though rarely, and then again in very different degrees of clearness) the thought flashes like lightning through the brain: " What is all this? or, *what* is its real nature? " The former question, in case it attains to great clearness and duration, will make the philosopher; and the latter, the artist or poet. The source of their high vocation, therefore, is the profound contemplation, arising, primarily, from the clearness with which they become aware of the world and of themselves. Hence, they are the wide-awake. The whole process, however, arises from the fact that the intellect, by its preponderance, frees itself temporarily from the will, to which it is originally subject.

The above reflections upon genius are supplementary to what has been put forth in the twenty-first chapter concerning the *continually wider separation of will and intellect,* perceptible throughout the chain of beings. This separation reaches its highest degree in genius, where it attains to the complete release of the intellect from its root, the will, so that the intellect here becomes wholly free, whereby, for the first time, the *world as representation* arrives at complete objectivation.

Still a few remarks touching the individuality of genius. Aristotle, according to Cicero (Tusc. 1, 33), has remarked that all geniuses were melancholy (*omnes ingeniosos melancholicos esse*), which, no doubt, refers to the passage in Aristotle's Problemata, 30, 1. Goethe, too, says:

> "Meine Dichtergluth war sehr gering,
> So lang ich dem Guten entgegenging:
> Dagegen brannte sie lichterloh,
> Wann ich vor drohendem Uebel floh.
> Zart Gedicht, wie Regenbogen,
> Wird nur auf dunkeln Grund gezogen:
> Darum behagt dem Dichtergenie
> Das Element der Melancholie."

This is to be explained from the fact that, the will always reasserting its original sway over the intellect, this, under unfavorable personal circumstances, more easily withdraws from them, because it gladly turns away from repulsive surroundings, as it were, to be diverted, and now turns with so much greater energy upon the strange outside world, that is, becomes more easily purely objective. Favorable personal relations have the opposite effect. On the whole, however, the melancholy given to genius rests upon the fact that the will to live beholds the wretchedness of its condition the more distinctly, the brighter the intellect is which illumines it. The frequently noticed gloomy disposition of highly gifted minds has its symbol in Montblanc, whose peak is usually clouded: but when, at times, especially in early morning, the cloud-veil is rent, and now the mountain, red with sun-light, looks down upon *Chamouni* from its heavenly height above the clouds, then it is a sight at which all hearts open in their lowest depths. So, too, genius, usually melancholy, shows, at intervals, that peculiar hilarity possible to him alone, arising from the most perfect objectivity of mind, and floating like an aureole on his lofty forehead; "*In tristitia hilaris, in hilaritate tristis.*"

At bottom, all bunglers are such, because their intellect, still too firmly bound to the will, becomes active only when spurred on by the will, and hence remains entirely in its service. They are, therefore, capable of none but personal purposes. Accordingly, their paintings are bad, their poems insipid, their philosophemes shallow, absurd, and very often dishonest, when, by pious dishonesty, they wish to recommend themselves to superiors. Thus, all their doing and thinking are personal. They succeed at best in making their own the external, the accidental, and the unimportant, that is, the manner of foreign, genuine works, so that instead of the kernel, they grasp the husk; but think they have achieved all, nay, to have surpassed those. If, in spite of everything, the failure becomes manifest, many still hope to reach it at last by their good will. But their good will itself makes it impossible, because it aims merely at personal purposes: these men, however, can have no sincere interest in art, or poetry, or philosophy. The saying: they stand in their own light, may well be applied to them. They do not suspect that only the intellect released from the sway of the will and all its projects, and so active of its own accord, inspires with true earnestness and enables to produce genuine works: and this is a blessing; otherwise they would drown themselves. In *morals, good will* is everything; but in art, nothing: where, as the very word indicates, nothing is valid save being able (können). In what a man is really *earnest*,— that is the final issue on which everything hinges. Nearly all persons are earnest exclusively in their own welfare and that of their kin; therefore, are able to further this and nothing else; just because no resolution, no voluntary and intentional exertion imparts or replaces, or, more properly, transfers the true, deep, real earnestness. For it always remains where nature has put it: without it, all can be but half accomplished. For the same reason, geniuses take but little care of their own welfare. As a leaden attachment always restores a body to that position which its center of gravity requires, so the true earnestness of a man always restores the power and attention of his intellect where his earnestness *lies:* anything else, man prosecutes *without earnestness*. Therefore, only those very rare, abnormal men, whose true earnestness lies not in the personal and practical, but in the objective and theoretical, are able to apprehend the essential qualities of things and of the world, that is, the highest truths, and reproduce them in any way. For such an earnestness, not concerned with the individual, lying in the *objective*, is something foreign to human nature, something unnatural, properly, supernatural: yes, without it, a great man is impossible, and, accordingly, his productions are then ascribed to a genius different from him, that takes possession of him. To such a man, his sculpturing, composing, and thinking are the *end;* to the others, a *means*. They seek to advance *their own interests*, and, as a rule, know well how to do it, for they accommodate themselves to their contemporaries, and are ready to serve their necessities and humors; hence, they generally live in happy, whilst he often lives in very miserable circumstances. For he sacrifices his personal welfare to the *objective* purpose: he can not do otherwise; because his earnestness lies there. They do the opposite: therefore, they are *little*, but he is *great*. Accordingly, his work is for all time; but it is not usually appreciated until his own generation has passed away. They live and die with the time. In general, he only is *great*, who, in his works, whether practical or theoretical, *seeks not his own interest*, but prosecutes an *objective* purpose: he is nevertheless great, even when, in practical matters, his purpose is misunderstood, and, in consequence, should be a crime. That he does *not seek to advance his own interest*, this makes him, under all circumstances, *great*. All action directed upon personal matters, however, is *little;* because the actor recognizes and sees himself only in his own infinitely small person. But the *great* man recognizes himself in everything and hence in the whole; he lives not like the former in the microcosm only; but even more in the macrocosm. Therefore, he takes an interest in the whole and endeavors to apprehend it, in order to represent, or to explain, or to practically influence it. For it is not foreign to him: he feels that it concerns him. On account of this extension of his sphere, he is called *great*.

Accordingly, this sublime predicate is due only to the true hero in any sense, and to the genius: it declares that they, in opposition to human nature, sought not their own interest, lived not for themselves, but for all. It is evident that the great majority must always be little and can never become great; however, the reverse is impossible, namely, for one to be great continually, that is, always and at every moment:

Denn aus Gemeinem ist der Mensch gemacht,
Und die Gewohnheit nennt er seine Amme.

Every great man must, nevertheless, often be a mere individual, keep an eye upon himself only, and that is to be *little*. Hereupon rests the very true remark, that no hero remains a hero to his valet; but it does not follow that the valet does not know how to appreciate the hero,—which Goethe, in the Elective Affinities, serves up as a thought of Ottilie's.

Genius is its own reward; for the best a man is, he must necessarily be for himself. "Who is born with a talent, to a talent, finds in it his fairest existence," says Goethe. When we look up to a great man of the past, we do not think: "How happy is he to be still admired by all of us," but: "How happy he must have been in the immediate enjoyment of a mind, by whose vestiges centuries are refreshed." Not in fame, but in what leads to it, lies the value, and in the generation of immortal children, the pleasure. Hence, those who endeavor to prove the nothingness of posthumous fame from the fact that the possessor knows nothing of it, are to be compared to the sophist who wisely demonstrates to a man casting envious looks at a heap of oyster-shells in his neighbor's yard, their utter uselessness.

In accordance with the above remarks about the nature of genius, it is contrary to nature, inasmuch as it consists in the emancipation of the intellect, whose real destiny is to serve the will, in order to be active of its own accord. Accordingly, genius is an intellect become unfaithful to its destiny. Upon this rest its concomitant *disadvantages*, to whose consideration we now pave the way, by comparing genius with less decided preponderance of intellect.

The intellect of the normal man, firmly bound to the service of his will, hence really engaged with the reception of motives only, may be looked upon as the collection of wires, whereby each of these dolls is set in motion upon the world's theater. This is the cause of that dry, grave earnestness of most persons, which is surpassed only by that of animals, that never laugh. But the genius, with his unshackled intellect, may be compared to a living man playing together with the great wire-dolls of the famous Milan puppet-show, who would among them be the only one perceiving all, and hence gladly separating himself for a while from the stage, in order to enjoy the play from the boxes: — this is the profound contemplation of genius. But even the very sensible and reasonable man, who might be called almost wise, differs from the genius very much; in fact, his intellect keeps a *practical* direction, is intent upon the choice of the very best ends and means; hence it remains in the service of the will, and is engaged in accordance with nature. The firm, practical earnestness, which the Romans called *gravitas*, presupposes that the intellect does *not* quit the service of the will in order to stray off to what does not concern it. Therefore, it does not permit that separation of intellect and will, by which *genius* is conditioned. The sagacious, nay, eminent mind, the one adapted to great achievements in practical matters, is such from the very fact that the objects strongly move his will and spur him on to a restless research of their relations. His intellect, too, is thus firmly grown together with his will. Before the mind of the genius, however, there floats in his objective apprehension the appearance of the world, as something strange to him, as an object of contemplation, driving his will out of his consciousness. Around this point turns the difference between the ability to accomplish *deeds* and to create *works*. The latter demands objectivity and depth of cognition, and presupposes a complete separation of will and intellect; the former, however, requires the application of cognition, presence of mind, and determination; this requires the incessant activity of the intellect, in the service of the will. Where the bond between the intellect and will is sundered, the intellect, having forsaken its natural destiny, will neglect the service of the will. For instance, even in the distress of the moment it will assert its emancipation and cannot refrain from catching the picturesqueness of the surroundings, though they threaten the individual with danger. But the intellect of the reasonable and sensible man is ever on duty, intent upon the circumstances, and their requirements: hence, the latter will, in all cases, resolve upon and execute what is proper to the occasion, consequently, never fall into any of those eccentricities, personal blunders, nay, follies, to which the genius is exposed, because his intellect remains not exclusively the leader and guardian of his will, but is more or less occupied with the purely objective. The opposite relation, in which these two entirely different kinds of ability, which have here been abstractly represented, hold to one another, Goethe has depicted in the contrast between Tasso and Antonio. The much observed relation between genius and insanity rests principally upon that separation of intellect and will, which is essential to genius, though contrary to nature. However, this must by no means be ascribed to genius being accompanied by less intensity of will; for it is conditioned rather by a violent and passionate character; but the explanation of it is that the man distinguished in practical matters, the man of deeds, has merely the whole and full measure of intellect necessary for an energetic will, while most people are defective even in this respect; genius, however, consists in a wholly abnormal, real surplus of intellect, not necessary for the service of any will. For this reason, men of genuine works are a thousand times rarer than men of deeds. It is in consequence of that very abnormal surplus of intellect, that the latter obtains a decided supremacy, separates itself from the will, and now, forgetting its origin, is spontaneously active by its own power and elasticity; whence arise the creations of genius.

Furthermore, the fact that genius consists in the activity of the free intellect emancipated from the service of the will, causes its productions to serve no useful purpose. Whether music, or philosophy, or painting, or poetry;—a work of genius is of no practical benefit. Uselessness is characteristic of the works of genius: it is their title to nobility; all other works of man are intended to preserve or to alleviate our existence—with the single exception of the works of genius: they are here for their own sake and are, in this sense, to be looked upon as the blossom, or net profit, of existence. Therefore, our heart opens when we enjoy them: for then we rise above the heavy, earthly atmosphere of want. Analogous to this, we seldom see the beautiful joined with the useful. Lofty and beautiful trees bear no fruit: fruit trees are small, ugly cripples. Not the full garden rose, but the small wild, almost scentless, rose is fertile. The most beautiful buildings are not useful: a temple is no dwelling-place. A man of great and rare mental endowments, forced to follow a mere useful business, for which the commonest man is fitted, resembles a precious vase, adorned with the most beautiful paintings, which is used for kitchen purposes. To compare useful people with geniuses, is to compare bricks with diamonds.

Accordingly, the merely practical man uses his

intellect for what nature intended it, that is, to apprehend the relations of things, partly to one another, partly to the will of the individual. Genius, however, uses it contrary to its destiny, to apprehend the objective, essential character of things. His mind, therefore, belongs not to him, but to the world, to whose enlightenment he will, in some way, contribute. Numerous *disadvantages* must result from this to the individual so favored. For his intellect will generally show those faults which are wont to be met with in every tool not used for what it was made. Primarily, it will be, as it were, the servant of two masters, as it quits at every opportunity the service for which it is destined, in order to prosecute its own ends; whereby it often leaves the will in the lurch very importunely; so that the individual thus endowed becomes more or less unfit for life, nay, often reminds us, in its behavior, of insanity. Besides, on account of its increased power of cognition, it will see in things more the general than the particular; while the service of the will requires principally the cognition of particulars. But when, at times, that entire, abnormally increased power of cognition suddenly throws itself, with all its energy, upon the affairs and miseries of the will, it will easily form too vivid a picture of them and behold everything in too glaring colors, in too dazzling a light, and magnified to an enormous degree; whereby the individual is driven to nought but extremes. The following may serve to elucidate this more fully. All great theoretical achievements, in what branch soever, are accomplished by the originator directing all the powers of his mind upon one point, on which he allows them to converge, and he concentrates them so strongly, firmly, and exclusively, that all the remaining world vanishes, and his object fills all reality. This great and powerful concentration, which is the privilege of genius, is, at times, directed also upon the objects of reality and upon affairs of daily life, which then, brought under such a focus, are so monstrously magnified that they appear like the flea taking the size of the elephant in the solar microscope. This accounts for the fact that highly gifted individuals sometimes, on account of trifles, break out into all sorts of fits of passion which are incomprehensible to others, who see them thrown into sadness, mourning, joy, anxiety, fear, rage, etc., by things that would have no effect whatever upon an ordinary man. Therefore, the genius lacks that *sobriety* which consists in seeing in things no more than what they really are, especially, as regards our possible purposes: hence no sober man can be a genius. With these disadvantages there is associated an excess of sensibility caused by an abnormally increased nervous and cerebral life, and concomitant with the violence and passionateness of the will, which are likewise conditions of genius, and which are physically manifested by the energy of the heart-beat. This is the source of that excessive tension of disposition, that violence of the emotions, that rapid change of humor, under predominating melancholy, which Goethe has depicted in *Tasso*. What reasonableness, composure, comprehensive oversight, complete certainty, and regularity of behavior are shown by the well endowed normal man, in comparison with the dreamy forgetfulness and passionate excitement of the genius, whose inner torment is the womb of immortal works. Furthermore, genius lives essentially in solitude. Too rarely it happens that he can ever easily find his like, and he is too different from the rest to be their companion. In them, will; in him, cognition, predominates: therefore, their pleasures are not his own; his pleasures, not theirs. They are merely moral beings and have merely personal relations: but he is also a pure intellect belonging as such to all humanity. The train of thought of the intellect severed from its maternal soil, the will, and only periodically returning to it, will soon be completely distinguished from the normal intellect clinging to its stem. For this reason, and because they cannot keep step with him, he is not fit to think in common, that is, to converse, with them. They will take as little pleasure in his crushing superiority as he takes in them; hence, they will feel more comfortable in the society of their like, and he will prefer the conversation with his like, although he can, as a rule, obtain this from their works only. Hence Chamfort has very truly remarked: "There are few vices which hinder a man as much as great qualities do, from possessing many friends." The happiest lot that can befall a genius is exemption from business, which is not his element, and leisure for his creations. From all this follows that, although genius can make its possessor very happy in the hours in which he is given up to it and revels unrestrained in its enjoyment, nevertheless, it is by no means adapted to render his life happy; rather, the contrary. This is confirmed also by the experience given in the biographies. Moreover, the genius is out of relation with the external world, because, in his very actions and achievements, he is usually in opposition to, and in battle with, his time. Mere men of talent always appear at the right moment: for, moved as they are by the spirit of their time, and called forth by its necessities, they are just about able to satisfy them. Hence they participate in the progressive course of their contemporary civilization, or in the gradual advancement of a special science: for this they receive reward and applause. But their works can no longer be relished by the next generation; they must be replaced by others that do not fail to appear. Genius, however, enters into his time like a comet into the orbits of the planets, to whose well regulated and easily discernible order, his wholly eccentric course is entirely strange. Accordingly, he cannot participate in the existing, regular course of the civilization of his time, but throws his works far ahead on the open highway (as the imperator consecrating himself to death throws his spear far ahead among the enemy), where time must overtake them. His relation to the men of talent flourishing at the time, he might express thus in the words of the evangelist: "My time is not yet come; but your time is always ready." (John 7 : 6.) *Talent* can perform what surpasses the ability of the others to achieve, though not their ability to apprehend : it, therefore, at once finds its appreciators. The work of the *genius*, however, transcends not only the ability of the others to accomplish, but also their ability to apprehend, it : hence these do not immediately become aware of it. Talent resembles an archer hitting a mark which the others cannot reach; genius resembles an archer hitting a mark which the others cannot even see. Therefore, they receive information about him, not immediately, but later on, and accept even this on mere faith. Accordingly, Goethe says in the *Indenture* : " Imitation is innate ; the master to be imitated is not easily recognized. Rarely is excellence found, still more rarely appreciated." And Chamfort says : "In respect to value, men are like diamonds. To a certain point of size, of purity, and of perfection, they have a fixed and marked price; but, beyond that point, they have no price and find no purchasers." Bacon of Verulam, too, has expressed it: "Common people praise the lowest, admire the mediocre, but have no sense for highest virtues." (*De Augm Sc.* L. VI. C. 3.) Yes, some one may exclaim, *apud vulgus!* Him, however, I must assist with Machiavelli's assurance: "*Nel mondo non e se non volgo.*" (In the world, there is nothing but rabble.) Philo, *On Fame,* remarks that usually one belongs more to the great mass than everyone thinks. It is in consequence of this late acknowledgment of works of genius, that they are seldom enjoyed by their contemporaries, and hence in the freshness of coloring which contemporariness and the present lend, but, like figs and dates, rather in a dry than in a fresh condition.

If, finally, we now consider genius from the somatic side, we find it conditioned by several anatomical and physiological qualities, any one of which is rarely found perfect, but still more rarely are they found all together, yet they are all absolutely necessary; so that it becomes clear, why genius occurs but as a wholly isolated, almost portentous, exception. The fundamental condition is an almost abnormal preponderance of sensibility over irribility and over the reproductive power, and, what heightens the difficulty, in a masculine body. (Women may possess considerable talent, but no genius: for they always remain subjective.) Likewise, the cerebral system must be utterly isolated from the ganglionic system, so that they are in complete opposition to one another. Thus the brain may lead its parasitic life upon the organism in a very decided, isolated, powerful, and independent manner. Thereby, indeed, it will easily have a hostile influence upon the rest of the organism and wear it out prematurely by its greater life and restless activity, if the organism itself be not likewise of energetic vital power and well constituted: the latter, therefore, is also one of the conditions. Nay, even a good stomach is necessary, because of the special and narrow consensus of this organ with the brain. Principally, however, the brain must be of unusual development and size, especially, broad and high: but the depth will be less, and the cerebrum will, in proportion, abnormally preponderate over the cerebellum. No doubt, much depends upon its shape as a whole and in its parts: but our knowledge is insufficient to determine this with exactness; although we easily recognize the noble form of a skull indicating great intelligence. The texture of the brain-mass must be of the highest degree of fineness and perfection, and consist of the purest, choicest, tenderest, and most irritable nervous substance: certainly, the quantitative relation of the grey to the white substance has a marked influence, which, however, we are not able to explain.

Moreover, from the post mortem examination of Byron's corpse, we know that the white stood in an unusually great proportion to the grey substance of the brain; likewise, that his brain weighed six pounds. Cuvier's brain weighed five pounds: the normal weight is three pounds. In comparison with the preponderating brain, the spinal cord and nerves must be unusually thin. A beautifully arched, lofty and broad skull of a thin osseous tissue must protect the brain without constraining it. This whole structure of the brain and nervous system is inherited from the mother; to which we shall return in the next book. However, this maternal inheritance is entirely insufficient to bring forth the phenomenon of genius, unless he inherits from the father an active, passionate temperament, manifested somatically as unusual energy of heart, and, consequently, of blood circulation, especially, towards the head. For thus, firstly, that turgescence peculiar to the brain, which causes the latter to press against its wall, is increased, so that, in case of fracture, it gushes forth from every aperture: secondly, by the due power of the heart, the brain receives that inner motion, still different from its constant rising and sinking at every respiration; it consists in a shock of its whole mass at every beat of the four cerebral arteries, whose energy must correspond to its here increased quantity. This motion is an indispensable condition for the activity of the brain. Therefore, a small stature, and especially a short neck are favorable to this activity, because the blood reaches the brain with more energy when the path is short: for this reason great minds rarely have large bodies. However, that shortness of distance is not indispensable: Goethe, for instance, was above the average height. But if all these conditions touching the circulation of the blood, which are inherited from the father, are wanting; the favorable structure of the brain inherited from the mother will produce, at best, a talent, a fine understanding, which is supported by the phlegm then appearing: but a phlegmatic genius is impossible. From this condition of genius coming from the father, many of the above described defects of temperament are to be explained. If this condition exists without the former, that is, together with an ordinary, or even ill-constructed, brain, the result is vivacity without intellect, heat without light, hotspurs, men of intolerable restlessness and petulance. That of two brothers, only one is a genius, and then usually the elder, as was, for instance, Kant's case, is, primarily, to be explained from the fact that only at *his* generation the father was at the height of strength and passion; although the other condition, received from the mother, may also be impeded by unfavorable circumstances.

I have yet to add a special remark about the *child-like* character of genius; that is, about a certain similarity between genius and childhood. During childhood, as well as in the genius, the cerebral and nervous system is decidedly preponderating: for its development far outruns the development of the rest of the organism; so that as early as the seventh year, the brain has received its full size and mass. Bichat, therefore, says: "In infancy, the nervous, compared with the muscular, system is proportionately greater than in all subsequent years, since from that time most of the other systems predominate over it. We know that in order to see the nerves distinctly infants are always taken. (*"De la vie et la mort."* Art. 8, Par. 6.) The genital system develops last, and not until the beginning of manhood are irritability, reproduction, and genital function in full power; and they then predominate over the mental function. From this it is to be explained that children, in general, are so sagacious, reasonable, fond of learning, and docile, nay, on the whole, fonder and fitter for all theoretical occupations than grown-up persons are: for, in consequence of that course of development, they have more intellect than will, that is, than inclinations, desires, passions. For, intellect and brain are one, and so is the genital system one with the most violent of all desires: hence, I have called it the focus of the will. For the very reason that the pernicious activity of this system still slumbers, while the brain is very active, childhood is the time of innocence and happiness, the paradise of life, the lost Eden, to which we, for the rest of our life, yearningly look back. The foundation of this happiness, however, is that in childhood our whole being lies much more in cognition than in will. This condition is still facilitated, by the novelty of all objects. Therefore, the world, in the dawn of life, lies before us so fresh, glittering so magically, so attractive. The petty desires, changeful inclinations, and trivial cares of childhood, are but a weak counterpoise to that predominance of cognition. The innocent and serene gaze of children, which delights us, and, at times, in a few, reaches the sublime, contemplative, expression with which Raphael has adorned the heads of his angels, is to be explained from the preceding. Accordingly, the intellectual powers develop much earlier than the necessities which they are intended to serve: and here, as everywhere else, nature acts very judiciously. For, at this time of predominating intelligence, man gathers a large supply of cognitions for future necessities, of which he is, at the time, still ignorant. Therefore, his intellect is now incessantly active, eagerly apprehends all appearances, broods over them, and carefully stores them up for a future time,—just as the bee gathers far more honey than she can consume, anticipating future necessities. It is certain that what a man gains in insight and knowledge until the age of puberty, is altogether more than all he subsequently learns, how learned soever he may become: for, it is the foundation of all human cognitions. Until this time, in the young body, plasticity predominates, whose powers later on, after it has completed its work, throw themselves, by a metastasis, upon the generative system, causing sexual instinct to appear along with puberty, and now the will gradually gets the supremacy. Following childhood, strongly theoretical, and fond of learning, is restless, now stormy, now melancholy, youth, which afterward passes over into violent and earnest manhood. Because that fatal instinct is wanting in the child, his will is so moderate and subordinate to cognition; whence arises that character of innocence, intelligence, and reasonableness, peculiar to childhood. I need hardly mention now wherein the similarity between childhood and genius consists: in the surplus of the powers of cognition over the wants of the will and in the predominance of mere cognition arising from it. In truth, every child is, to a certain extent, a genius, and every genius, to a certain extent, a child. Their affinity is shown, primarily, in the naiveté and sublime simplicity which is a fundamental trait of the true genius: it is also manifested in many other traits: so that a certain childlike character indeed belongs to the genius. In Riemer's notes on Goethe, it is mentioned that Herder and others censured Goethe, that he was ever a great child: they certainly remarked, but did not blame, it with justice. Of Mozart, too, it was said that he remained all his life a child. (Nissen's Biog. of Mozart, Page 2 and 529.) Schlichtegroll's Necrology (of 1791, Vol. II: Page 109) says of him: "He became, at an early age, a man in his art; in all other relations he remained forever a child." Every genius is a great child, truly because he gazes into the world as into something strange, a play, therefore, with purely objective interest. Accordingly, he has as little as the child that dry earnestness of common people, who, capable of no other than subjective interests, always see in things mere motives for action. Who does not remain all his life a great child, but becomes an earnest, sober, sedate, and reasonable man, can be a very useful and able citizen of this world; but nevermore a genius. Indeed, he is a genius from the fact that, abnormally, he retains all his life that preponderance of the sensible system and of cognition natural to childhood; so that this preponderance becomes perennial. Truly, a trace of it continues in many ordinary men to the period of youth; so that, for instance, in many students, an aspiration still purely intellectual and a genial eccentricity are unmistakable. But nature falls back into her old track: they metamorphose and arise in manhood as philistines incarnate, who terrify us, when we meet them again later in life. Upon the preceding rests Goethe's fine remark: "Children do not fulfill what they promise; young people very seldom, and when they keep their promise, the world does not keep its word with them." (Elective Affinities,

Part I: Chap. 10.) And that world places the crowns, which it raised up on high for merit, on the heads of those who become the tools of her base intentions, or know how to deceive her. In accordance with what has been said, there exists, besides a mere youthful beauty, which nearly all, at sometime, possess (*beauté du diable*), a mere youthful intellectuality, a certain spiritual being, inclined and adapted to apprehend, understand, and learn. Everyone has it in childhood; few, in youth; but like the youthful beauty it is soon lost. Only in very few, the select, the one as well as the other continues during life so that, even at an advanced age, a trace of it is still visible: these are the truly beautiful and the true men of genius.

The preponderance of the cerebral nervous system and of intelligence during childhood, and its retrogression in mature age, which have been considered, receive important elucidation and confirmation from the fact that in the *genus* which ranks next to man, the monkey, the same relation is found to exist in a striking degree. It has gradually become certain that the highly intelligent ourang-outang is a young Pongo, who, as soon as he is grown up, loses the great similarity between his and the human face and, at the same time, the astonishing intelligence, in that the lower, animal, part of the face enlarges the forehead, in consequence, recedes, large *cristæ* for the development of the muscles give his skull an animal shape, the activity of the nervous system sinks, and, in its stead, an extraordinary muscular power is developed, which, being sufficient for his preservation, now renders his great intelligence useless. Of especial importance is what has been said in this respect by Frederick Cuvier, and elucidated by Flourens in his review of the former's · *Histoire Naturelle;* this review is to be found in the September number of the *Journal des Savans*, of 1839, and is separately reprinted with several additions under the following title: *Résumé analytique des observations de Fr. Cuvier, sur l' instinct et l' intelligence des animaux, p. Flourens*, 1841. He says (p. 50): "The intelligence of the ourang-outang, an intelligence so highly and early developed, decreases with age. While the ourang-outang is young, he astonishes us by his sagacity, by his cunning, and by his address. But the adult ourang-outang is nothing but a gross, brutal, intractable, animal. This is the case with all monkeys as well as with the ourang-outang. In all of them, intelligence decreases in proportion as their strength increases. The animal which has most intelligence, has all of it in youth only." Furthermore, (p. 87): "Monkeys of all kinds offer this inverse relation of age and intelligence. Thus, for example, the *entellus* (a kind of she-monkey of the sub-*genus* of the *symno-pithecus*, and one of the monkeys venerated in the religion of the Brahmanists) has, in youth, a large forehead, the snout projecting somewhat, and an elevated, rounded skull, etc. With age, the forehead recedes, the snout becomes prominent, and his moral changes no less than his physical nature: apathy, violence, love of solitude take the place of sagacity, docility, and confidence." "These differences are so great," says M. Cuvier, "that, accustomed as we are to judge the actions of animals by our own, we would take the young animal for an individual of the age in which all the moral qualities of the species are acquired, and the adult *entellus* for an individual who had nothing but his physical strength. But nature does not act thus with animals that must not leave their appointed sphere. It is sufficient for animals to be in some manner able to preserve their existence. For this, intelligence was necessary as long as there was no strength; and as soon as this was acquired, all other powers lost their utility." And p. 118: "The preservation of the species depends no less upon the intellectual than upon the organic qualities of animals." The latter confirms my doctrine that the intellect, as well as claws and teeth, is nothing but a tool for the service of the will.

ÆSTHETICS OF POETRY.

AS the simplest and most correct definition of poetry, I would call it the art of exciting by words the power of the imagination. How this is brought about, I have shown in the first volume, § 51.* A special confirmation of what has been said, is furnished by the following passage from a letter of Wieland to Merck: " I have spent two days and a half upon a single stanza, where the matter really depended upon a single word which I wanted and could not find. I twisted and turned the matter and my brain in all conceivable directions; because, of course, where a picture is at stake, I would gladly bring the same definite vision that is floating before my mind, before the mind of my readers too; and for which, as you know, all frequently depends upon a single stroke or turn." (Letters to Merck, edited by Wagner, 1835, Page 193.) Because the reader's imagination is the material in which poetic art represents its pictures, this has the ad-

---

* "Die Welt als Wille und Vorstellung."

vantage that the more special execution and finer traits so appear in each one's imagination, as is at the time most suitable to his individuality, his sphere of cognition, and his humor, and hence affects him in the most lively manner; the plastic arts, however, cannot thus accommodate themselves, but here *one* picture, *one* figure, must suffice for all; but this will, in some respect, always bear the stamp of the individuality of the artist or of his model, as a subjective, or accidental, ineffective addition; although the less, the more objective, that is, the more of a genius the artist is. Even from this it may partially be explained, that the works of poetry exercise a much stronger, deeper, and more general influence than pictures and statues: for these usually leave people entirely cold. And, after all, the plastic are the least effective arts. An odd proof of this is furnished by the frequent discovery of the pictures of great masters in private houses and all sorts of places, where, for centuries, they have hung, not indeed buried, and hidden, but merely unnoticed, consequently, without effect. In my own time (1823) there was discovered in Florence even a Madonna of Raphael, which had, for many years, hung on the wall of the servant's room in a palace (in the *Quartiere di S. Spirito*): and this happens in Italy, a nation endowed more than all others with sense of beauty. It proves how little direct and immediate effect the works of the plastic arts have, and that appreciation of them needs, far more than that of all others, education and knowledge. But how infallibly a beautiful melody touching the heart travels around the world, and an excellent poem wanders from people to people. That the great and rich lend powerful aid merely to the plastic arts, and bestow considerable sums upon *their* works; nay, that to-day an idolatry, in the real sense of the word, gives the value of a large estate for a picture of a renowned old master, is caused principally by the rarity of the masterpieces, whose possession, therefore, suits their pride; but also because their enjoyment requires very little time and exertion, and is ready every moment for a moment; while poetry, and even music, involve much more troublesome conditions. Accordingly, the plastic arts may be wholly missed: whole nations, for example, the Mohamedan, are without them: but there is none without music and poetry.

Now, the purpose the poet has in setting our imagination in motion, is to reveal to us the ideas, that is, to show by an example what life and the world are. To do this he must, in the first place, know himself what they are: accordingly, his poetry will prove deep or shallow according to the depth of his cognition. Thus, just as there are unnumerable gradations of depth and clearness in the apprehension of the nature of things, so are there of poets. Each one of them, however, must consider himself excellent in so far as he has correctly represented what *he* intuitively knows, and in so far as his picture corresponds to the original: he must place himself on a footing of equality with the best poets, because he recognizes no more in their pictures than in his own, viz: as much as in nature herself; for his vision penetrates no deeper. The best poet, however, recognizes himself as such in that he sees how shallow the vision of the rest was, how much there lay back of it, which they could not reproduce because they did not see it, and how much farther his vision and his picture reach. If he understood the shallow poets as little as they understand him, he would have to despair: for, because it takes quite an extraordinary man to do justice to him, and common poets can esteem him no more than he does them, he must feed a long time on his own applause before the world's follows. Meanwhile, even his own applause is impaired, because they expect him to be very modest. But it is as impossible for him, who has merits and knows what they cost, to be blind to them himself, as for a man six feet high not to know that he overtops the others. If the distance from the base to the top of a tower is three hundred feet, the distance is certainly as great from the top to the base. Horace, Lucrece, Ovid, and nearly all ancient writers have spoken proudly of themselves; likewise, Dante, Shakespeare, Bacon of Verulam, and many others. To be a great mind without being impressed by it, is an absurdity which only disconsolate inability would endeavor to believe, in order to regard the feeling of its own worthlessness as modesty also. An Englishman made the witty and true remark, that merit and modesty have nothing in common save the initials*. I always entertained a suspicion that modest celebrities may be right in their opinion of themselves, and Corneille says, unreservedly:

"La fausse humilité ne met plus en credit:
 Je scais ce que je vaux, et crois ce qu'on m'en dit."

(False modesty gives no one more credit:
 I know what I am worth, and believe what they tell me of it.)

Goethe, finally, candidly says: "Only scamps are modest." But, more infallible still would be the assertion that those who so zealously demand modesty from others, urgently press for modesty, and incessantly cry: "Modesty, for God's sake, modesty!" *are assuredly scamps*, that is, wholly worthless wretches, nature's factory-ware, regular members of the mass of mankind. For whoever possesses merits himself, admits them also in others, — of course, genuine and real merits. But he who is destitute of all excellencies and merits, wishes there were none at all: the sight of them in others puts him on the rack: pale, green, sallow envy

---

* According to Lichtenberg, Stanislaus Lescinsky said: "Modesty ought to be the virtue of those who lack the others."

consumes his heart: he would annihilate and extirpate all who are personally endowed; but, if he unfortunately must let them live, it is to be solely under the condition that they hide, wholly deny, yes, abjure their superiority. This, then, is the source of the frequent eulogies on modesty. And when the extollers of it have an opportunity to extinguish merit in the cradle, or at least to prevent its display, who will doubt that they do it? For this is the practice to their theory.

Although the poet, like every artist, always presents to our view only the particular, the individual; yet, what he perceived, and wishes us to perceive, thereby, is the (Platonic) idea, the whole genus, so that in his images, as it were, the type of human characters and situations will be expressed. The narrative, as well as the dramatic, poet selects from life the wholly particular, and depicts it exactly in its individuality, but reveals thereby our entire human existence: for, though seemingly engaged with particulars, he is in reality engaged with what exists everywhere and at all times. This accounts for the fact that sayings, especially of the dramatic poets, though not necessarily general opinions, find frequent application in practical life.

Philosophy holds the same relation to poetry as empirical science to experience. For experience gives us, by examples, an acquaintance with single phenomena; science embraces the whole, by means of general ideas. Thus, the object of poetry is to acquaint us with the Platonic ideas of beings, by means of particular things and by examples: the object of philosophy is to teach us to see the inner essence of things as a whole, and in general which is revealed in them. Even from this it may be surmised that poetry bears more the character of youth; philosophy, more that of age. In fact, the poetic gift blooms in youth only;—also, the susceptibility to poetry is often passionate in youth: a youth takes delight in verses as such, and is often satisfied with mediocre productions. With age, this inclination gradually declines, and in old age prose is preferred. By that poetic tendency in youth, the sense of reality is often corrupted. For the difference between this and poetry is, that, in the latter, life glides along painless and yet interesting; in the real world, however, life, as long as it is painless, is uninteresting, but, as soon as it becomes interesting, it is not without pains. The youth who is initiated into poetry prior to reality then demands from the latter, what the former alone can do for him: this is the chief source of that discomfort depressing the most excellent youths.

Metre and rhyme are fetters, but likewise a garment which the poet throws about him and under which he is allowed to speak as he otherwise could not: this is what delights us. Indeed, he is but half responsible for what he says: metre and rhyme must answer for the other half. Metre or the measure of time has, as mere rhythm, its essence in *time* alone, which, is a pure intuition, *a priori*, hence belongs, in Kant's language, solely to *pure sensibility;* however, rhyme is a mere matter of sensation in the organ of hearing, that is, of *empirical* sensibility. Hence rhythm is a far nobler and worthier aid than rhyme, which the ancients accordingly disdained, and which took its origin in the incomplete languages that arose, in barbaric times, by the corruptions of the ancient languages. The poverty of French poetry rests chiefly upon the fact that, being without metre, it is restricted to rhyme; and is, moreover, increased by the fact that, in order to hide its want of means, it has made rhyming more difficult by a multitude of pedantic rules, for instance, that only syllables written alike rhyme, as though it were for the eye, not for the ear; that the hiatus is proscribed; many words dare not occur, etc., all of which the modern French school of poets endeavors to put an end to. In no language, at least for myself, does rhyme make so strong and pleasant an impression as in the Latin : the medieval rhyming Latin poems have a peculiar charm. It must be explained from the fact that the Latin is without comparison more perfect, beautiful, and noble than any modern language; so that it marches so gracefully in the ornaments and tinsel belonging to the latter, but disdained by the former.

To serious consideration, it would appear almost high treason against reason if the least violence were done to a thought, or even to its correct and pure impression, with the intention to hear the same sound again after a few syllables, or also to have these syllables themselves represent a certain jingle. But without some violence, few verses make their appearance: for to this it must be ascribed that, in foreign languages, poetry is much more difficult to be understood than prose. Could we glance into the secret work-shop of the poets, we would find ten times oftener that the thought is sought for the rhyme, than that the rhyme is sought for the thought: and even in the latter instance, the issue is not without concession on the part of the thought. Yet the art of versification defies these considerations, and has all times and peoples on its side: so great is the power which metre and rhyme exercise over our feelings, and so effective is their peculiar, mysterious *lenocinium*. I would explain this from the circumstance that a happily rhymed verse, by its indescribably emphatic effect, rouses the sensation that the thought expressed in it had lain predestined, nay, preformed in the language, and the poet had but to search it out. Even trivial thoughts receive from rhythm and rhyme a touch of significance and cut a figure in this ornament, as, among maidens, ordinary faces fascinate the eye by finery. Nay, even erroneous and entirely false thoughts acquire a show of truth by versification. On the contrary, even famous passages from renowned poets shrink up and become insignificant, when faithfully translated into prose. If the true alone is beautiful and the greatest ornament of truth is nakedness, then a thought appearing beautiful in prose will have more true value than one equally effective in poetry. That a means like metre and rhyme, seemingly so trivial, nay, childish, should exercise such an effect, is very striking and well worth investigation. I explain it in the following manner: That which is immediately given to the ear, that is, the mere sound of words received from rhythm and rhyme, is a certain perfection and significance in itself; for it then becomes a kind of music: accordingly, it seems now to exist for its own sake and no longer as a mere means, a mere sign of something signified, that is, of the sense of the words. To delight the ear with its sounds, seems its whole destiny, and, having done this, everything seems to be accomplished and every claim satisfied. That it, at the same time, conveys a meaning, expresses a thought, proves, as it were, an unexpected addition, like the words to music, an unexpected gift, pleasantly surprising us, and, because we made no claims of this sort, very easily satisfying us: but if this thought is one which, as such, that is, expressed in prose, would be significant, we are charmed. I can remember from early childhood that I found pleasure in the pleasant sound of verses, before I made the discovery that they contained throughout meaning and thought. Accordingly, there may exist in all languages a sort of ding-dong poetry, almost entirely destitute of meaning. The sinologist, Davis, in the preface to his translation of the *Laou-sang-urh*, or, An Heir in Old Age (London, 1817), remarks that the Chinese dramas consist in part of verses that are sung, and adds: "Their meaning is often obscure, and, acccording to the statement of the Chinese themselves, the special purpose of these verses is to flatter the ear, whereby the meaning is neglected and frequently, perhaps, wholly sacrificed to harmony." Who is not reminded here of the choruses of many Greek tragedies often so difficult to be deciphered?

The sign whereby the genuine poet of higher as well as of lower rank is most immediately known, is the spontaneity of his rhymes; they came, as it were, by divine dispensation: his thoughts come to him in rhymes. The secret prosaist seeks a rhyme for the thought; the bungler, the thought for the rhyme. From a rhyming couplet, we can very often find out to which verse the thought, and to which the rhyme, is father. The art consists in hiding the latter that such verses may not appear as mere *bouts-rimés*.

My feeling of the matter (proofs cannot be given) is, that rhyme, from the nature of it, is merely secondary: its effect is limited to the single return of the same sound, and is not strengthened by frequent repetition. Accordingly, as soon as a final syllable has perceived the one of like sound, its effect is exhausted: the third return of the sound has but the effect of another rhyme, accidentally hitting the same sound, but without heightening the effect: it is joined to the preceding rhyme without, however, producing a stronger impression. For the sound of the first syllable does not continue thus through the second to the third: the latter is an æsthetic pleonasm, a double courage that is of no assistance. Therefore, such accumulations of rhymes are least deserving of the heavy sacrifices which are the price of ottaverimes, terzerines and sonnets, and which are the cause of that soul-torture, frequently inflicted upon us by reading those productions: for poetic enjoyment, while your brains are in the rack, is impossible. The fact that a great poetic genius can sometimes overcome even those forms and their difficulties, and move about with ease and grace is no compliment to them, for as such, they are as ineffective as troublesome, and even when good poets make use of these forms, we frequently see the battle between the rhyme and the thought where now the one, now the other, gains the victory; that is, either the thought is mutilated for the sake of the rhyme, or the latter is compromised with a feeble *à peu près*. I take it for a proof not of ignorance, but of good taste, that Shakespeare, in his sonnets, has given other rhymes to each of his quatrains. At any rate, their acoustic effect is thus not in the least diminished, and much more justice is done to the thought than would have been the case, if he had rigidly laced it in the traditional Spanish boots.

It is a disadvantage to any poetry for the language to have many words not used in prose, and, again, certain words which cannot be used in poetry. The former occurs oftenest in the Latin and Italian, the latter, in the French, where it recently was very strikingly designated as *la bégueulerie de la langue Française* (the prudery of the French language): both are to be found less in the English and least in the German. Words belonging exclusively to poetry are foreign to our hearts, do not speak to us, and so leave us cold. They are a conventional language of poetry, and, as it were, merely painted, instead of real feelings. They exclude true sincerity (Innigkeit).

The difference between *classic* and *romantic* poetry, so often discussed in our day, seems to me to rest, at bottom, on the fact that the former knows no motives other than the purely human, real, and natural: the latter, however, adds artificial, conventional, and imaginary motives: to these belong those whose origin dates back to the Christian mythus; secondly, those of the chivalrous, overstrained, and fantastical principle of honor; furthermore, those of the stale and ridiculous Christian-Germanic woman veneration; finally, those of prating and moonstruck hyperphysical love. To what grotesque distortions of human relations and of human nature these motives may lead, may be seen even in the best poets of the Romantic school, Calderon, for instance. Not to mention the Autos, I call to mind but such plays as *No siempre el peor es cierto* (Not Always is the Worst Certain) and *El postrero duelo en España*, (The Last Duel in Spain), and similar comedies *en capa y espada:* in addition to these elements, there are associated the frequently prominent scholastic subtleties in conversation, which then belonged to the mental culture of the higher classes. How advantageously does the poetry of the ancients, always remaining true to nature, compare with it. It follows that classic poetry has an absolute, the romantic, but a relative, truth and correctness, analogous to Greek and Roman architecture. However, we must remark that all dramatic or narrative poems placing the scene of action in ancient Greece or Rome stand at a disadvantage, because our knowledge of antiquity, especially what concerns the details of life, is insufficient, fragmentary, and not derived from intuition. For this forces the poet to evade a great deal and to resort to generalities, whereby he wanders into the abstract, and his work loses that intuitive character and individualization which are absolutely essential to poetry. This it is, which gives to all works of that sort the peculiar tinge of voidness and tediousness. Only Shakespeare's representations of that class are free from it, because, under the name of Greeks and Romans he has unhesitatingly represented Englishmen of his time.

Many masterpieces of lyric poetry, especially several odes of Horace (for instance, the Second Ode of Book III), and several of Goethe's songs (as The Shepherd's Lament), have been criticised for lacking the proper connection and abounding in sudden leaps of thought. But here the logical connection has been intentionally neglected to be replaced by the unity of the fundamental feeling and mood expressed therein; which, on that very account, become more prominent, in that they pass like a string through the separate pearls, and so mediate the rapid change of objects of contemplation; as in music, the transition from one key to the other is mediated by the heptachord, by which the fundamental tone continuing the sound in it becomes the dominant of the new key. The quality here described is found more distinctly, indeed, to excess, in the song of Petrarch, beginning with the words:

Mai non vo' piu cantar, com' io soleva.

As in lyric poetry the subjective element predominates, so in the drama, on the contrary, the objective, is the sole and exclusive element. Between both, epic poetry, in all its forms and modifications, from the narrative romance to the epic proper, occupies a broad intervening space. For, although it is in the main objective, it yet contains a subjective element, becoming more or less prominent, which is manifested in the tone, in the form of the discourse, as well as in the interspersed reflections. We never lose sight of the poet so completely as we do in the drama.

The object of the drama, in general, is to show us by an example what the essence and existence of man are. The poet may here display the sad or the cheerful side of it, or, their transition stages. But the very expression "essence and existence of man" contains the germ of the controversy, whether the essence, that is, the characters, or the existence, that is, fate, event, action, is the main point. Moreover, both are so firmly grown together, that the idea, but not the representation of them may be separated. For only circumstances, destinies, events, bring the characters to reveal their nature, and only from characters arises action, from which there spring events. Of course, in the representation, the one or the other may be made the more prominent: in this respect, the character-play and the intrigue-play constitute the two extremes. The purpose common to drama and to epic, namely, to represent eminent characters in striking situations and the extraordinary actions brought about by both, will be most perfectly accomplished by the poet, if he first shows us the characters in a state of rest, in which merely their general coloring becomes visible, but then allows a motive to enter causing an action from which a fresh and stronger motive arises; this calls forth a more important action, which, in turn, begets new and continually stronger motives; thus, in a space of time adapted to the form, there enters, in place of the original quiet, passionate excitement, in which the important actions occur, by means of which the qualities previously slumbering in the characters, together with the course of the world, are revealed.

Great poets metamorphose themselves entirely into each of the persons to be represented, and speak from each of them like a ventriloquist, now, in the character of the hero, and then again in that of the young, innocent maiden, with equal truth and naturalness: so Shakespeare and Goethe. Second-class poets change the chief person to be represented into themselves; so Byron's, whereby often the other persons remain without life; as in the works of the mediocre, the chief person too.

The pleasure we take in *tragedy* belongs not to the feeling of the beautiful, but to the feeling of the sublime; indeed, it is the highest degree of this feeling. For, as we, at the sight of the sublime in nature, abandon the interest of the will, in order to be in a state of pure contemplation;

so, in the presence of the tragical catastrophe, we abandon the will to live itself. For, in the tragedy, the terrible side of life is brought before us, the misery of mankind, the sway of chance and of error, the fall of the just, the triumph of the wicked: that is, the condition of the world, forever combating our will, is displayed. At the sight of this, we feel summoned to avert our will from life, to desire and love it no longer. But in consequence of this, we become aware that there is then something else left of us, which we can never know positively, but merely negatively, as something which desires life no longer. As the heptachord requires the fundamental chord, as red requires green, and even produces it in the eye, so every tragedy requires an entirely different existence, another world, a knowledge of which can be given us only indirectly, as in this case by such a demand. At the moment of the tragic catastrophe, we are more strongly than ever convinced that life is a heavy dream from which we must awake. To this extent the effect of tragedy is analogous to the dynamically sublime, in that tragedy, like the latter, elevates us above the will and its affairs, and so changes our feeling that we feel pleasure in the very things which repel us. What gives to all tragedy, in what shape soever it may appear, the peculiar impetus to exaltation, is the dawning cognition that the world, that life can offer no true satisfaction, consequently, are not worthy of our attachment; therein consists the tragical spirit; it, therefore, leads to resignation.

I grant that in the tragedy of the ancients this spirit of resignation is seldom directly prominent and expressed. Œdipus Colonus, it is true, dies resignedly and willingly; but revenge upon his native country consoles him. Iphigenia of Aulis is very willing to die; but it is the thought of Greece's welfare that consoles her and causes the change in her feeling, in consequence of which she willingly accepts the death she at first wishes to escape in every possible way. Cassandra, in the Agamemnon of the great Æschylus, dies willingly, αρκειτω βιος. 1308; but she too is consoled by the thought of revenge. Hercules, in the Trachiniæ, yields to necessity, dies calmly, but not resignedly. The same holds true of the Hippolytus of Euripides, where we are struck by the fact that Artemis, who comes to console him, promises him temples and fame, but does not at all point to an existence after life, and forsakes him in death, as all gods forsake the dying: in Christianity, they approach the dying, and so, too, in Brahmanism and Buddhism; though, in the latter, the gods are really exotic. Thus, Hippolytus, like most of the tragic heroes of the ancients, shows submission to inevitable fate and to the inflexible will of the gods, but no surrender of the will to live itself. As Stoic indifference is fundamentally different from resignation, because the former teaches but patient endurance and calm expectation of inevitably necessary evils; Christianity, however, surrender of the will; so the tragic heroes of the ancients show steadfast submission to the inevitable blows of fortune; Christian tragedy, however, the surrender of the entire will to live, joyous departure from the world, in the consciousness of its worthlessness and nothingness. But I am entirely of the opinion that the modern tragedy ranks higher than the ancient. Shakespeare is far greater than Sophocles : compared with Goethe's, the Iphigenia of Euripides might appear almost rude and vulgar. The Bacchantes of Euripides are a revolting fabrication in favor of the pagan priests. Many ancient plays have no tragic tendency whatever, as the Alceste and the Iphigenia of Taurus of Euripides: some have repugnant or even nauseous motives, as the Antigone and the Philocletus. Nearly all their plays show mankind under the atrocious rule of chance and error, but not the resignation caused by, and delivering from, it. And all because the ancients had not yet attained the summit and goal of tragedy, indeed, of the view of life in general.

Accordingly, if the ancients but little represent the spirit of resignation, the will's abandoning life, in their tragic heroes themselves, as their sentiment; it, nevertheless, remains the peculiar tendency and effect of tragedy to awaken that spirit in the spectator and call forth, though but temporarily, that feeling. The terrors of the stage display to him the bitterness and worthlessness of life, the vanity of all his striving: it must be the effect of this impression that he, if but in vague feeling, perceives that it were better to tear his heart away from life, to avert his will from it, not to love life and the world; whereby, then, in the inmost depths of his nature, the consciousness is aroused that, for a different kind of will, there must be another kind of existence. But, if this were not the case, if the tendency of tragedy were not exaltation above all the aims and terrors of life, this abandonment of it and of its allurements and the turning to another existence, though wholly incomprehensible to us — how could it at all be possible that the representation of the terrible side of life, brought before us in the most glaring light, could exercise a beneficent effect and become a source of high enjoyment to us? Fear and pity, which are, according to Aristotle, the final object of tragedy, do, forsooth, not belong to the pleasant emotions; hence they cannot be the object, but only a means. Thus, the summons to avert the will from life remains the true tendency of tragedy, the final object of the intentional representation of the sufferings of mankind, and is it still, where the resigned exaltation of spirit is not shown in the hero himself but merely roused in the spectator at the sight of great sufferings of which the hero was guiltless, nay, even at the sight of those of which he was guilty. As the ancients, so, too, many of the moderns are content with putting the spectator into that feeling by the objective representation of human misery at large; while others represent in the hero himself the revolution produced by suffering: those give, as it were, only the premises and leave the conclusion to the spectator; while these give the conclusion or the moral of fable too, in the shape of the revolution of the hero's feelings, or, perhaps, even as reflection in the mouth of the chorus; as, for instance, Schiller, in The Bride of Messina: "Life is not the highest of possessions." I may remark here, that the genuinely tragic effect of the catastrophe, that is, the hero's resignation and the exaltation of mind brought about by the catastrophe, is seldom so purely motived and clearly expressed as in the opera *Norma*, where it appears in the duet *Qual cor tradisti, qual cor perdesti*, in which the revolution of the will is clearly indicated by the sudden calmness of the music. In general, this piece, considered apart from its excellent music, as well as from its diction, which can be but the language of an opera,— and considered solely according to its motives and inner economy, is a highly perfect tragedy, a true model of tragic arrangement of motives, of tragic progress of action, and of tragic development, together with its world-elating effect upon the feeling of the hero, which then, likewise, takes possession of the spectator: indeed, the effect here attained is so much the more unequivocal and expressive of the true essence of tragedy, as neither Christians nor Christian sentiments occur in it.

The neglect of the unity of time and place, for which the moderns have been so frequently criticised, becomes a fault only when it goes so far as to destroy the unity of action: in this case, there remains only the unity of the chief persons, as, for instance, in Shakespeare's Henry VIII. The unity of action, however, need not go to such an extreme that continually the same subject is discussed, as in the French tragedies, which so strictly observe it that the course of the drama resembles a geometric line without breadth; the watchword is always, "Go ahead!" *Pensez à votre affaire,* (mind your own business!) and the matter is dispatched and settled in a very business-like manner, and non-essentials are not allowed to detain it. Shakespeare's tragedy, however, resembles a line that has breadth too: it takes time, *exspatiatur:* there occur speeches, even entire scenes, which do not advance the action, even do not really concern it, but from which we learn to know more intimately the acting persons or their circumstances, so that we then understand the action more thoroughly. This, it is true, is the main point; but not so exclusively that we should forget that the object, in the last instance, is the representation of human nature and of life in general.

The dramatic or epic poet ought to know that

he is fate, and, therefore, to be as inexorable as the latter;—likewise, that he is the mirror of mankind, and, therefore, he ought to allow very many bad, at times, desperate characters, to appear, as well as many silly persons, distorted minds, and fools, but now and then, a reasonable, a sagacious, an honest, a good, and only, as a rare exception, a noble, man. In all Homer, there is, I think, not one really noble character represented, although some very good and honest ones : in all Shakespeare there may be, at all events, a few noble, though by no means exceedingly noble characters, perhaps Cordelia, Coriolanus, hardly more. However, his plays are swarming with the kind described above. But the plays of Iffland and Kotzebue have many noble characters, while Goldoni has done as I have recommended; whereby he shows that he takes a higher rank. Lessing's Minna von Barnhelm, labors strongly in too much and universal nobleness. But so much nobleness as is to be found in that one Marquis Posa, is not to be gathered from Goethe's complete works taken together. There is, however, a short German play, *Duty for Duty* (a title seemingly taken from the Critique of Practical Reason), which has but three persons, yet all three of exceeding nobility.

The Greeks, as a rule, took royal personages as the heroes of their tragedies; the moderns, for the most part, also. Certainly not because rank gives more dignity to the actor or sufferer : and, since the sole object is to set human passions in motion, the relative value of the objects, by which this is brought about, is indifferent; so that farmyards and kingdoms serve equally well. Yet the tragedy of common life is by no means to be entirely rejected. Persons of great power and authority are best adapted to tragedy, because the unhappiness, in which we are to recognize the fate of human life, must be of sufficient magnitude to appear terrible to the spectator, whoever he be. Euripides, himself says: φευ, φευ, τα μεγαλα, μεγαλα, Και πασχει κακα. Now, the circumstances which put an ordinary family into distress and despair, are, in the eyes of the great or rich, usually very trivial and to be redressed by human efforts, nay, frequently by a trifle; these spectators, therefore, cannot receive a tragic impression from them. But the misfortunes of the great and powerful are positively terrible and inaccessible to outside assistance; for kings must help themselves by their own power or perish. And besides, the fall is greater from the greater height. Common persons, accordingly, want height to fall from.

Now, if we have found as the tendency and last object of *tragedy* a tendency to resignation, to the denial of the will to live, we will easily recognize in its counterpart, the *comedy*, the summons to continued affirmation of the will to live. It is true that comedy, as every representation of human life, must display sufferings and reverses;

but it shows them to us as transitory, dissolving into pleasure, generally mixed with success, victory, and hope, which finally preponderate; and thus it affords many opportunities for laughter, with which life, nay, adversity itself, is filled, and which, under all circumstances, is to keep us in good humor. It declares that, in the end, life on the whole is very good and entertaining throughout. Of course, comedy must make haste to drop the curtain in the period of pleasure, that we may not see what follows; while tragedy, as a rule, so closes that nothing can follow. And, if we but once take a serious view of that burlesque side of life, how it is displayed in the naive expressions and gestures which petty disconcertedness, personal fear, momentary anger, secret envy, and many similar fits of passion impress upon the figures of reality, that depart considerably from the type of beauty; — from this side, too, the pensive observer may unexpectedly become convinced, that the existence and actions of such beings cannot be here for their own sake; that they, on the contrary, entered existence upon a wrong path; and that what so represents itself had better not be.

EDUCATION.

IN accordance with the nature of our intellect, ideas ought to arise by means of the power of abstraction from intuitions; whence it follows that the latter ought to precede the former. Now if this course is really followed, as in the case of him who has only his own experience as teacher and book, he knows very well what intuitions are included under each of his ideas and are represented by them: he is intimately acquainted with both and accordingly treats everything he meets with properly. We may call this course natural education. In artificial education, on the other hand, the head, by means of dictation, teaching, and reading, is crammed full of ideas, before there is any extensive acquaintance with the real world. Now, experience is expected afterward to supply all those ideas with intuitions, but till then, the former are misapplied, and things and men, accordingly, wrongly judged, wrongly seen, wrongly treated. Thus it happens that education produces warped minds, and thence it comes that in youth, after long years of study and reading, we enter the world often partly foolish, partly perverse, and conduct ourselves at one time timidly, at another foolhardy, because we have the head full of ideas which we are now anxious to apply, but almost always misapply. This is the result of that *hysteron proteron* by which we, in direct opposition to the natural course of mental development, receive ideas first and intuitions last; because educators, instead of developing in the boy the ability to know, judge, and think for himself, take pains merely to cram his head with foreign, ready-made thoughts. Afterward a long experience must correct all those judgments that have arisen from a false application of ideas. This is rarely a complete success. Therefore so few scholars have that sound common sense so frequently found among the unlearned.

In accordance with what has been said, the essential point in education is that the *acquaintance with the world*, to obtain which we may denote as the object of all education, should begin at the right end. But this rests, as has been shown, principally upon the fact that in every case the intuition precede the idea; furthermore, that the narrower come before the wider idea, and so the entire instruction occur in that order in which the ideas of things presuppose each other. As soon, however, as a link is omitted in this chain there arise defective, and from these, false ideas, and finally, a distorted view of the world clinging to everyone a long time, to the most, forever. Whoever examines himself, will discover that about some quite simple things and relations the right or clear understanding came to him not until a very mature age and, sometimes, on a sudden. Then there lay here a dark spot in his knowledge of the world that had arisen by skipping the object in his early education, be it an artificial one or merely a natural one from his own experience.

Accordingly, the real, natural order of the succession of cognitions ought to be explored in order to acquaint children methodically with the facts and relations of the world, without getting flaws, often not to be expelled, into their minds. Here care must be taken that children do not use words with which they associate no definite idea.*

The principal thing, however, is that intuitions should precede ideas and not the reverse as is the usual case, but just as unfavorable as when a child enters the world legs first, or poetry, rhyme first. While, however, the child's mind is very poorly supplied with intuitions, ideas and judgments, really prejudices, are already being incul-

---

* Even children very often have that unfortunate tendency, instead of endeavoring to understand the thing, to content themselves with words, and get these by heart, in order to get themselves out of difficulty when occasion calls. This tendency continues in after life and causes the knowledge of many scholars to be merely verbal rubbish.

cated : this ready apparatus he afterward applies to intuitions and experience, instead of the former growing out of the latter.

The world of intuitions is many sided and rich and cannot, therefore, compete in brevity and rapidity with the abstract idea, that is soon done with everything. For this reason, it will bring to an end the correction of such prejudiced ideas only very late, or never. For whichever side experience may show forth as contradicting a prejudice, its declaration will forthwith be rejected as one sided, even denied, and eyes closed against it, only that the bias may not run the risk of damage. So it happens, then, that many a man carries about with him all his life, flaws, whims, fantasies, and prejudices that approach fixed ideas. For he has never tried to abstract for himself thorough ideas from intuitions and experience because he has received everything ready-made. This it is which makes him, makes innumerable men, so flat and shallow. Instead of this, therefore, the natural course of education should be retained. No idea, unless based upon an intuition, ought to be introduced into the mind, at least not without verification. In this case the child would receive few but thorough and correct ideas. He would learn to measure things by his own, instead of a foreign standard, and would never acquire a thousand whims and prejudices, to drive out which the best part of life and experience must be sacrificed. His mind would forever be accustomed to thoroughness, clearness, discrimination, and fairness.

In general, children should learn to know life in every respect not any sooner from the copy than from the original. Therefore, instead of merely hurrying to put books into their hands, they ought rather to be made acquainted, step by step, with things and human relations. Above all, care must be taken to lead them to a clear conception of reality, and so to educate their minds that they will always draw their ideas immediately from the actual world, and form them according to reality, instead of getting them from other sources, as books, fables, or the talk of others, and afterwards, applying notions thus acquired to reality. The latter, then, they, with their head full of chimeras, partly falsely apprehend, partly endeavor in vain to model after those chimeras, and so fall into theoretical, or even practical errors. For it is incredible how much harm early implanted chimeras, and prejudices arising from them, cause. The later education, which the world and real life give us, must then be principally devoted to eradicate them. Hereupon rests the answer of Antisthenes reported by Diogenes Laertius (VI, 7): When asked what was the most necessary learning, he replied: "To unlearn evils."

For the very reason, that early imbibed errors are usually not to be rooted out, and the power of judgment is the last to come to maturity, children, until their sixteenth year, should be exempt from all subjects wherein great errors are possible, that is, from philosophy, religion, and general views of every description, and prosecute such studies only wherein no errors are possible, as in mathematics, or none are very dangerous, as in languages, science, history, etc.; in general, however, at every age only such sciences as are accessible and wholly intelligible. Childhood and youth is the time to gather data and to learn to know single things, specially and thoroughly. General judgments, on the other hand, must still be suspended, and final explanations postponed.

The power of judgment presupposing, maturity and experience ought still to rest, and not be anticipated by ingrafting prejudices which cripple it forever.

Memory, however, since it has its greatest strength and tenacity in youth, is preëminently to be cultivated, but with the most careful discrimination. For, since that which has been well learned in youth, clings forever, this precious gift should be used to the greatest possible advantage. If we consider how deeply sunk into our memory are the persons we have known in the first twelve years of our life, and how, too, the events of that period, and nearly all which we then experienced, heard, and learned are inirradicably impressed upon it, it is a very natural thought to base education upon this plasticity and tenacity of the young mind by regulating all impressions upon it strictly methodically and systematically according to direction and rule. But as only a few years are allotted to man and the capacity of the memory in general, and still more that of the individual memory is limited, everything depends upon filling it with the most essential and important facts in every department, exclusive of everything else. This selection should be made with due consideration by the ablest minds and masters in every branch, and its result determined. It must be based upon what is necessary and important to know for man in general, and what for every trade and profession in particular. The knowledge of the first class would then have to be divided into graded courses or encyclopædias, according to the amount of general culture allowed to each one by his worldly circumstances, from limitation to the most necessary primary instructions to all the studies of the philosophical faculty. In the second class, however, the choice of what is necessary would be left to the true masters in every branch. The whole would give a fully detailed canon of intellectual education which, of course, would require a revision every ten years.

By such a preparation the power of memory in youth would be utilized to the greatest advantage, and provide the later appearing power of judgment with excellent material.

The maturity of cognition, that is, the perfection

to which it can attain in each one, depends upon the close connection between all his abstract ideas and his intuitions, so that each one of his ideas rests mediately or immediately upon a direct intuition, by which alone they have real value; and likewise, that he is able to class any intuition under the right and appropriate idea. Maturity is the work of experience and, consequently, of time only. For since we gain our intuitive and abstract cognitions usually separately, the former in the natural way, the latter, through the good or bad instruction and information of others, there is in youth rarely much agreement and connection between our ideas fixed by mere words and our real knowledge derived from observation. Both approach each other very gradually, and mutually correct each other. But not until they have entirely grown together does there exist maturity of cognition. This maturity is wholly independent of the greater or less perfection of his other faculties, as these do not depend upon the relation between his abstract and intuitive cognition, but upon the original intensity of both.

For the practical man, the most necessary study is the acquisition of an exact and thorough knowledge of worldly affairs. But it is also the most tedious study, since it continues until old age, without the whole field being surveyed, while in the sciences, we master the most important facts even in youth. In that knowledge, the boy and youth, as novices, have to learn the first and hardest lessons; but often even the man of ripe years has much to make up in it. This difficulty, considerable in itself, is doubled by the reading of romances which picture events and men as they really are not. These, however, are received with the credulity of youth and incorporated into the mind; whereby, in place of mere negative ignorance, there enters a whole web of false suppositions as positive error, which afterwards confuses even the school of experience and causes its teachings to appear in a false light. If the youth was previously in the dark, he is now led astray by wandering will-o'-the wisps: with girls it is frequently even worse. By novels an entirely false view of life is forced upon them, and expectations are roused that can never be satisfied. This exerts one of the most baneful influences upon their whole life. Persons who have in their youth no time or opportunity to read novels, as tradesmen and the like, have decidedly the advantage here. A few novels are to be excepted from this reproach, nay, rather produce an opposite effect, especially Gil Blas, and other works of Lesage (or rather their Spanish originals), The Vicar of Wakefield, and some of the novels of Walter Scott. The Don Quixote may be regarded as a satirical representation of these very errors.

www.ingramcontent.com/pod-product-compliance
Lightning Source LLC
Chambersburg PA
CBHW032157160426
43197CB00008B/955